Student-Focused Learning

Student-Focused Learning

Higher Education in an Exponential Digital Era

Edited by
Darrel W. Staat

ROWMAN & LITTLEFIELD
Lanham • Boulder • New York • London

Published by Rowman & Littlefield
An imprint of The Rowman & Littlefield Publishing Group, Inc.
4501 Forbes Boulevard, Suite 200, Lanham, Maryland 20706
www.rowman.com

6 Tinworth Street, London SE11 5AL, United Kingdom

Copyright © 2020 by Darrel W. Staat

All rights reserved. No part of this book may be reproduced in any form or by any electronic or mechanical means, including information storage and retrieval systems, without written permission from the publisher, except by a reviewer who may quote passages in a review.

British Library Cataloguing in Publication Information Available

Library of Congress Cataloging-in-Publication Data
Names: Staat, Darrel W., 1941- editor.
Title: Student-focused learning : higher education in an exponential digital era / Edited by Darrel W. Staat.
Description: Lanham : Rowman & Littlefield, [2020] | Includes bibliographical references.
Identifiers: LCCN 2020007906 (print) | LCCN 2020007907 (ebook) | ISBN 9781475854978 (cloth) | ISBN 9781475854985 (paperback) | ISBN 9781475854992 (epub)
Subjects: LCSH: Student-centered learning. | Educational technology. | Social media in education.
Classification: LCC LB1027.23 .S79 2020 (print) | LCC LB1027.23 (ebook) | DDC 371.39/4—dc23
LC record available at https://lccn.loc.gov/2020007906
LC ebook record available at https://lccn.loc.gov/2020007907

Contents

Preface		vii
Acknowledgments		xi
Introduction		xiii
1	Concept-Based Education *Linda Latham*	1
2	Project-Based Education *Maria Williams*	19
3	Online Education *Donald Miller*	37
4	The Flipped Classroom Education *Darrel W. Staat*	55
5	Gaming Education *Melisa Johnson*	67
6	YouTube Education *Antonio Jefferson*	83
7	Google Education *Cameron Jackson*	99
8	MOOC Education *Angela Davis*	117
9	Virtual Reality Education *Darrel W. Staat*	133

Epilogue	141
About the Editor	143
About the Contributors	145

Preface

As the 21st century proceeds year by year, it is obvious that the effects of Moore's Law are exponentially impacting the development of computer power. A single transistor placed on a chip the size of the thumbnail in 1957 has expanded to the equivalent of 100 billion transistors, which can be placed on that same size chip in 2019. That is hard to fathom, but it's true.

Expansion from one to 100 billion transistors on a chip in a mere 62 years created all kinds of possibilities. Ideas become realities almost immediately. In just a few years, Facebook served billions around the world. In less than a decade, Uber became the largest people transportation system in the world, and Airbnb developed into the largest room service organization in the world. Computer power, algorithms, and computer storage made the growth of those organizations and others possible. As a result, social media expands, the taxi business changes, and the hotel industry has new competition.

Today, technologies such as 3D printing, autonomous vehicles, drones, the Internet of Things, personal robots, genome development (medical and agricultural), Bitcoin/Blockchain, nanotechnology, artificial intelligence, and quantum computing are developing in a linear manner, (stage one), preparing for an exponential explosion, (stage two), in the near future. They are not going to develop in a linear manner like aircraft in the 20th century from the Wright brothers in 1903 to today's jets and rockets. Rather, they are going to develop like Facebook, Uber, and Airbnb. One day they begin as an idea, a few short years later they are in full operation. Watch quantum computing, which Google has developed in 2019 and stand back as it impacts the digital world.

As people live in this exponential era, they will try to get used to it. It will take effort to become comfortable with the digital technologies that increase in ferocious velocity far beyond what was normal in the 20th century. Most likely some kind of reasonable transition will be achieved. The younger generation will be attracted to the changes and accept them easily. The older generation will move more slowly in acceptance; however, the benefits will soon demonstrate to all that using the technologies makes good sense.

3D printing will become as normal as using a personal computer. Instead of typing words, the printer will construct just about anything in relatively short order. Autonomous cars will make more time available when traveling and will significantly reduce highway accidents. The internet of things will make living easier; personal robots will assist humans at work and home, and genome development will address illness with significant successes leading to healthier, longer lives and produce agricultural products to meet the increasing needs of a growing population. Cryptocurrency and Blockchain will provide alternative methods of banking and contracts. Artificial intelligence will support life in a multitude of ways; quantum computing will stand classical computing on its head, and nanotechnology will bring unlimited products to the consumer.

As the new technologies burst upon the scene in their exponential stage one area, so important to civilization, will most likely be dragging on behind, higher education. The lecture/discussion method of teaching will be continued by the faculty of community colleges and universities. The argument will most likely be that it worked for the Greeks and has continued to work well throughout history as the way to educate human beings; so, there is no need to change now.

However, external to higher education, the business community is observing the development of the digital technologies and is looking for ways to incorporate the technologies into their businesses. They know, if they choose to ignore the technologies, their competition will not. The business world understands that changes in technologies will produce methods and processes that will help them improve their products, reduce costs, and increase profits. They will soon be looking to community colleges and universities to assist them in incorporating the technologies and training the workforce needed.

In addition, 21st-century students will be enrolling in higher education with full expectations that the technologies they are aware of and already have been using will be part and parcel of the education processes. They will expect that the faculty and staff of community colleges and universities will be well informed and competent in using the digital technologies. They will expect to see teaching methods that use the technologies and allow the student to learn in ways different from the traditional lecture/discussion method.

As a result of the needs from the business community and the expectations from the student population, teaching methods in higher education will need to change significantly. The focus of this book is to provide the faculty, staff, and administration with methods that will suit both the expectations of the

21st-century student and the needs of the business community. New methods are emerging and others further developing that will make significant contributions to the new normal in higher education. Incorporating them into the teaching/learning process will become absolutely necessary.

This book gives educators a view into the kinds of methods that will make sense to use in the 21st century. Higher education will need to make a transition from what is accepted practice today, to what will become successful methods in the near future. In short, the emphasis will be on placing the student in the center of the educational process. Teachers and professors will play an entirely different role in the near future. It is best to be prepared rather than falling behind, or worse, caught completely off-guard.

Acknowledgments

I would like to express my appreciation to my colleagues at Wingate University who have shown interest in my work and encouraged me to continue. They are truly a superb team to work with.

I would like to thank Dr. Charlesa Hann, assistant dean of the Graduate Education, at Wingate University. She has provided an understanding of the work it takes to research and write a book such as this and the encouragement to continue for the benefit of all concerned.

In addition, I want to thank the graduate students in Cohort Six of the Higher Education Executive Leadership program at Wingate for their interest, time, and effort to make this book possible.

Finally, I express my sincerest appreciation to my wonderful wife Beverly who has grown used to the time and effort it takes for research and writing. Her support is of inestimable value to me.

Acknowledgments

Introduction

In *Understanding Media: The Extensions of Man*, Marshall McLuhan stated, "the medium is the message" (McLuhan, 1964, p. 23). His insight into the future of what he called the electronic age was impressive. He envisioned a future in which everything was going to change as the result of the coming electronic age (McLuhan, 1964). His statement that the medium is the message has rung true over the decades.

In 2019 more technologies than that McLuhan envisioned are currently developing. By 2050, most of them will be accepted as normal for human beings on the earth, and wherever else they may have moved to in the galaxy. As the technologies developed, they changed in the way humans understood life, culture, and the universe itself. Looking forward to the next few decades, it will become obvious that the way education is provided will need to be significantly modified from that currently in use.

McLuhan's notion of the medium is the message that applies to teaching methodology in the 21st century. How the teaching medium occurs will be the message to the student. If it is done in ways that reflect the past, the method will be unattractive to the student. Two of my grandsons were born after 2000. One is in college this fall. He has worked with computers since age three. He has played video games since age five. He owns an iPad and an Apple Watch and uses social media. He and his fellow students will want to learn in a student-centered manner using digital technologies.

The chapters in this book describe methods that can be used to successfully work with the upcoming generation of community college and university students. Each chapter provides information, ideas, and concepts that can be put into use today in anticipation of what will be required in the near future. The sage-on-the-stage with lecture/discussion method will gradually die down over the next decade to be replaced with the learning manager. If the lecture method remains in the future, it will probably be used in formal or procedural settings. In the community college and university, it will be replaced by methods more suitable to learning for the technology-savvy student and the digitally developing businesses.

Learning methods for the 21st century will include those which are student-centered, learning-focused, and digitally enhanced. Teaching will become learning management; the lecturer will become a learning manager; and students will become learning inventors. That kind of change may not make everyone in education today happy, but the expectations of the student and the needs of the business community will guide the ultimate direction of the future learning process.

This book provides chapters describing a number of methods to be used in higher education in the 21st century. Some methods have been in existence for a period of time; others are literally at the front edge of development. All have possibilities for success when working in the digital world. Trying them out, piloting them, and experimenting with them for the benefit of the student and business community is well worth the effort.

It is best to be as prepared as possible for future changes rather than waiting to see what is going to happen. Those who try and are successful will be the leaders in learning management of the near future. Those who hold back will find themselves in the most difficult position of playing catch up in a digital world that moves forward with exponential velocity. In the digital world, being at the leading edge has definite advantages.

This book can be used by 21st-century educators in community colleges and universities to learn what methods already exist that differ from the traditional lecture/discussion method. Further, faculty can begin to try out the various methods to see what works best for them and their subject matter. No matter which method is used, the connecting thread is focusing on the student as learner with the faculty member as a learning guide.

To survive in the 21st century, students will need to become continuous learners, developing with the high-paced changes that they face. Educators will need to keep this critical concept in mind as they develop their teaching methods. For the 21st century, when developing the teaching/learning methods, the instructor must remember that the medium is the message in the learning process.

Chapter 1

Concept-Based Education[1]

Linda Latham

Teaching and learning theories are ever-evolving processes. Characteristics of learners, as well as supporting bodies of knowledge, change over time. In order to prepare graduates for an ever-increasingly complex and "globally interdependent world," educators must ground their style and pedagogy in "cognitive science, learning theory, and the commonsense reasoning of what works in teaching and learning" (Erickson, Lanning, & French, 2017, p. 1).

Colleges and universities have long been known for teaching in large lecture hall types of environments, with the *sage-on-the-stage*. College professors have had the reputation of having a teaching philosophy of *if I don't say it, they can't learn it* and that they have to cover all knowledge on the subject at hand for a college course to be complete. What we now know about how learning occurs lends itself to examine how traditional higher education teaching occurs.

Concept-based curricula are not new to education, but are not necessarily widely used and understood in postsecondary settings. Secondary educational settings have been discussing what concepts are and how to facilitate their understanding for some time. A concept is considered to be "a mental construct that frames a set of examples sharing common attributes" and "one or two-word concepts are timeless, universal, abstract, and broad" (Erickson, 2002, p. 164).

Concept-based education moves the learner to a higher level of abstraction, utilizing synergistic thinking which in turn "leads to deeper understanding of facts, skills, and concepts" (Erickson & Lanning, 2014, p. 11). To understand how to teach conceptually, one must first examine learning theories related to conceptual learning.

LEARNING CONCEPTUALLY

Conceptual learning is multidimensional. It is an active, synergistic learning process with a highly engaged learner that facilitates higher level, critical thinking (Giddens, Caputi, & Rodgers, 2015). It typically builds from a starting point of knowing to deeper understanding in the learner.

Constructivism

Concept-based curricula have their roots in constructivist learning theory, in which the learner connects new information to previously gained knowledge (Fletcher et al., 2019). In this way, the learner is constructing a mental scaffold of connected information, knowledge, and experiences. If they have no related knowledge, then learners construct a new cognitive framework to hold this different information. Knowledge is constructed by the learner, rather than by the teacher (O'Banion, 1997).

Conceptual learning is closely related to constructivism in that both philosophies view context as an enhancement to the learning process. Learning is seen to be experiential, creating meaning from past experiences and environmental interactions (Fletcher et al., 2019). Many students prefer to learn ideas and concepts in the context of a real-life application situation; for example, often students ask how could algebra skills and knowledge possibly assist them later in life?

Additionally, conceptual learning "takes the learning one step further, creating transfer of knowledge to future unknown situations and contributes to future responses of the learner" (Fletcher et al., 2019, p. 11). This feature allows the learner to continue to build on information long after a course has concluded.

Constructivism supports student motivation by virtue of having more interaction with the learning (Juvova, Chudy, Neumeister, Plischke, & Kvintova, 2015). Students are active, with both mental and psychomotor skills. And, most students will tell faculty that they are hands-on learners; "human beings learn best by doing" (O'Banion, 1997, p. 41). Whether in K–12 settings or in college classrooms, faculty would likely agree that deep understanding of information is facilitated by the learner being able to manipulate and experiment with it, whether cognitively or physically. The more a learner can experience the information, the more they truly know it.

Conceptual Learning Process

Conceptual learning can take place when information is gained actively, contextually, and centered on the learner (Giddens, 2007). It is not necessarily linear, but is organized in a logical fashion for the learner, and the new information is connected to either previous knowledge or experiences. According to Fletcher et al., "conceptual learning is a process in which learners organize concept-relevant knowledge, skills, and attitudes to form logical cognitive connections resulting in assimilation, storage, retrieving, and transfer of concepts to applicable situations, familiar and unfamiliar" (2019, p. 9). Learners form linkages from the new information to previously learned concepts.

In conceptual learning, individuals "recognize patterns in information" and subsequently search for where similar information is stored in their brain (Fletcher et al., 2019, p. 9). The learner then forms connections with previously acquired knowledge. Once this connection is made, the learner can take the new concept to a deeper level and begin to cluster information. The new information then becomes personal as its relevance is discovered and applied to new situations (Fletcher et al., 2019).

Conceptual Learning in Educational Settings

Ascribing to the characteristics of conceptual learning leads the educator to use instruction that fosters a deep level of learning, rather than memorization of unrelated facts for upcoming exams. "Memorization does not create deep understanding because context is often absent" (Fletcher et al., 2019, p. 12).

New topics are actually more interesting to students when they hold relevance to knowledge previously acquired. When subjects are interesting and relevant to students, they tend to be more motivated to learn. Faculty in higher education crave that their students would love to learn and would learn to think critically. Encouraging conceptual learning to take place is a viable way for this to happen.

Disciplines that have quickly evolving knowledge bases are perfect for making use of conceptual building blocks. Healthcare disciplines, such as nursing and physical therapy, have realized that their graduates will need to continue to evolve and add to their knowledge long after graduation. They cannot remain relevant in their profession if they only memorize procedures and facts. They have cited their own curricula with "content saturation," and the need to provide students with a way to learn vast amounts of changing information while preparing them for future changes in healthcare (Giddens, 2007, p. 65).

Children and young adults can learn conceptually, as well. As young learners are building their knowledge base, they can construct mental models that build connections early on. These connections can help the child to rapidly build on current knowledge. Teachers in K–12 settings have already realized that their young students are more engaged and retain information beyond the test when deeper, conceptual learning has taken place.

TEACHING CONCEPTUALLY

Since conceptual learning is an active learner style, it stands to reason that the strategies employed by educators would contain active learning strategies. These strategies may be rather different from what faculty, particularly in higher education, have been used to. They would vary greatly from the way that most faculty themselves were taught. Most faculty were taught by the sage-on-the-stage in a lecture hall type of format. Active learning lessons are quite different, both for the teacher and for the student.

Components of Concept-Based Instruction

H. Lynn Erickson has done much of the current research and writing on concept-based education, and contends that there are four essential components, "synergistic thinking, the conceptual lens, inductive teaching, and guiding questions" (Erickson & Lanning, 2014, p. 95). Erickson notes that conceptual teaching is three-dimensional, adding concepts to the already two-dimensional instruction of facts and skills that is familiar to most educators (Erickson & Lanning, 2014). The third dimension allows the student to see the facts and skills learned to come alive, be applied to real situations, and be seen in context of their meaning.

Synergistic Thinking

Synergy is created when deeper understanding occurs with the learning of facts and skills. Knowledge of facts and skills requires a lower-level cognitive process, while deeply understanding the related concepts is a much higher level of cognition. Combining the two requires "a more sophisticated curriculum and instruction model" and supports "developing the students' ability to think well in order to solve complex problems and create new ideas" (Erickson & Lanning, 2014, p. 10). The result is a higher level of thinking and processing of new information for students.

Conceptual Lens

The conceptual lens can be applied to a unit title or theme by broadening the learning out to transcend "time, across cultures, and across situations" (Erickson & Lanning, 2014, p. 99). For example, a science unit on plants could transform with a conceptual lens to become a unit on adaptation. A history unit on World War II could become a unit on leadership and power (Erickson & Lanning, 2014).

In this way students can learn concepts that they can apply to other, perhaps similar, situations. They can apply the facts to a broader, overarching concept.

Understanding of the concept then relates to other concepts that the student recognizes. When patterns and connections are realized, "we can understand the deeper, transferable significance of our learning, then we can say our thinking is *integrated* at a conceptual level" (Erickson et al., 2017, p. 15).

Inductive Teaching

Inductive teaching utilizes the practice of discovery. The premise of the unit of study is not necessarily spelled out up front, but rather, discovered as the students learn and "build meaning for themselves" (Erickson & Lanning, 2014, p. 99). The unit could begin with a question rather than a statement of fact, for example. This type of teaching helps to develop the skill of inquiry and critical thinking. The understanding is actually drawn from the students, instead of meaning being given to them from the beginning (Erickson & Lanning, 2014). This skill can then continue to learning in the future.

Guiding Questions

Guiding questions help the learner to move through both facts and concepts related to the content. Facts are important, but are locked in time or place, whereas "conceptual questions transfer through time, across cultures, and across situations, just as concepts transfer through time, across cultures, and across situations" (Erickson & Lanning, 2014, p. 102). Students can learn information from both factual and conceptual types of questions to guide their inquiry.

Other questions to add to student discussions might be open-ended debate questions, for which there is "no right or wrong answer and are intellectually engaging and interesting" (Erickson & Lanning, 2014, p. 103). Each of these four components (synergistic thinking, the conceptual lens, inductive teaching, and guiding questions) serves to enhance student learning and stimulate excitement around learning.

Facts and Skills

One area of trepidation for educators is that teaching conceptually may overlook the facts in a topic or a discipline. According to Erickson et al. (2017), "facts and skills are critical to conceptual understanding. One cannot understand a concept, or conceptual idea, without factual and skill support" (p. 120). Facts and skills are building blocks for the learners to assemble the framework "for hooking new knowledge onto prior conceptual structures in the brain" (p. 121). Further exploration into concept-based, curriculum-building resources would be necessary for those faculty designing the new pedagogy.

CURRENT PRACTICES IN K–12 CLASSROOMS

In kindergarten through the 12th grade, educators are teaching conceptually, perhaps calling it problem-based instruction, unit themes, mindful learning, or big ideas. They have already implemented active learning strategies in order to keep students engaged and to meet state and national curriculum standards.

Primary and Elementary Grades

Very young children can learn from each other and begin to see relationships within concepts that they study; for example, kindergarten children learning shapes make a hexagon from other shapes, rather than simply learning a list of unrelated shapes (E. Moore, personal communication, June 7, 2019). In learning from each other, students can see how others make connections in their minds. They can then apply the same method to their own learning process. Children can build a stronger foundation of knowledge, rather than simply memorizing facts for a test by exploring conceptual ideas (E. Moore, personal communication, June 7, 2019).

Older elementary-aged children might study the concept of change through a problem-based learning activity and inquiry-based exploration in a science lesson where they examine a pond ecosystem. To develop such a unit of study, a pair of sixth-grade teachers used "an overarching idea to provide a conceptual lens through which students view[ed] the content of a particular subject" (Schill & Howell, 2011, p. 40). The teachers chose a topic (ecology), selected the concept of change, and decided on a problem-based learning activity as a focus for the unit. The teachers used inquiry-based investigations to support the students' learning as the students made generalizations from their research (Schill & Howell, 2011).

High School

Some teachers organize content around a vision or a big idea. For example, a tenth-grade English concept might be social justice issues within literature (M. Alston, personal communication, June 13, 2019). One would still teach the factual literary devices, but would soon move to themes and concepts that students could explore more freely and deeply.

Another high school English teacher aims to make the stories, literature, and history relatable to her students. But rather than checking off a list of the classics that every student must read, followed by a test of their reading comprehension and knowledge of the characters and literary terms, she uses the literature as a vehicle for delivering concepts (C.K. Smith, personal communication, June 21, 2019).

The literature can then come alive in a relevant, contemporary way in order to "convey useful, universal themes related to societal issues, to make us better people" (C.K. Smith, personal communication, June 21, 2019). Classic, timeless writings become tools to convey patterns in behavior and human tendencies rather than isolated, well-written stories (C.K. Smith, personal communication, June 21, 2019).

It would seem that high school math would be taught using strictly facts and formula memorization, but to the contrary, one math educator explains:

> When students have not yet mastered the prerequisites or skills needed, you can't teach them in isolation. You have to scaffold them into conceptual understanding. You cannot isolate conceptual understanding from procedures and applications because they have to understand why. An example of a concept would be that students need to be able to conceptualize that when you add polynomials you are adding like terms which requires the skill of adding integers, so if a student does not understand the concept, they will struggle with adding polynomials; however, you shouldn't teach a full day on integers. You would incorporate a piece like integers into a larger concept like polynomials. Once they understand the concept of adding like terms, you can unpack a skill like adding integers. Once they see it as a concept interconnected to other skills, they can apply the skills to other situations. (A. Foggie, personal communication, July 13, 2019)

Once they have the conceptual understanding, they can apply it to several situations. Conceptual understanding involves procedural fluency and application, but conceptual is the why.

A lot of math teachers stay at procedural level without giving them the why. But once they have the conceptual understanding they can transfer the skills to application which means they can apply the skill in multiple situations, even "real-world" applications (A. Foggie, personal communication, July 13, 2019).

Even math, history, science, and language arts can transform learning to conceptual understanding. Bringing real-life context to learning activities can increase the conceptual processing and application (Erickson, 2002). All learners, whether children or adults, are encouraged in their learning when information is practical and applicable to their lives.

CURRENT PRACTICE IN HIGHER EDUCATION

Concept-based practices can be found in higher education, from adult basic skills to advanced health science curricula, as well as others. Disciplines where high engagement is desired and where vast amounts of knowledge are changing quickly are looking to concept-based curricula.

Adult Basic Education

Moving away from the mundane repetitive skills practice, other pedagogies are being explored in adult basic education programs. Such strategies as "problem-based learning and concept maps as evidenced-based opportunities to foster basic and higher-order thinking skills" (Smith, 2014, p. 51) have been recommended. These teaching strategies offer to contextualize learning into something relevant to the adult student. Once again, the result is a more engaged, active learner who connects "new concepts with old familiar concepts" (Smith, 2014, p. 53). Deeper learning occurs among individuals, as well as learning from more group interaction. Hence, learning is active, rather than passive.

Health Sciences

The 21st century ushered in several calls at the national level for educational reform in nursing and other healthcare disciplines, citing content overload as well as complex, dynamic healthcare environments as driving forces (Giddens et al., 2008). Health science disciplines have struggled with content saturation, as educational programs are challenged with equipping entry level practitioners with vast amounts of ever-changing health-related *and* discipline-specific knowledge (Giddens & Brady, 2007).

This saturation can be attributed to "the information age, changes in health care delivery, and the ongoing teacher-centered approach to teaching" (Giddens et al., 2008). All of the information must be ingrained into the graduates' daily practice rather than simply memorized, or even learned for an exam. Classroom and theoretical knowledge must be transferrable and applicable to their clinical experiences (Graham, 1996).

An example of dealing with this heavy content dilemma is seen in physical therapy education, which has shifted from competency-based to problem-solving to problem-based reflective learning, drawing from constructivist learning theory (Graham, 1996). In one study, students who used fact memorization "without understanding the larger context of the material generally found that they were unsuccessful" (Graham, 1996, p. 864).

Students in the study kept journals as to their thoughts and reactions throughout selected physical therapy courses. Interestingly, these students "often used visualization as a method of gaining a holistic understanding of the concept without memorizing the details" (Graham, 1996, p. 864). Visualization is a useful strategy in a learner-centered approach.

Nursing has been at the forefront of recent progress with concept-based curricula in higher education. Building on the work of Erickson, faculty within the field of nursing have effectively made the case for teaching nursing in a conceptual manner. Advantages to arranging the curriculum around key nursing concepts include better content management and critical thinking promotion (Giddens et al., 2008).

Academic concept-based curricula have built around a comprehensive list of essential concepts pertinent to the discipline and validated in the literature. This practice helps to prevent unnecessary repetition and organizes the concepts in a logical sequence (Giddens & Brady, 2007).

Proponents of concept-based curricula in nursing have advocated active learning strategies such as concept maps, games, unfolding case studies, virtual web-based case study learning platforms, and high fidelity simulation. Each of these strategies allows the student to apply factual information learned from textbook readings or class lectures to contextual reality-based scenarios.

Some, such as the unfolding case study and simulation allow the scenario to evolve as it would in real-life situations and allows the students to think it through and to respond. There is also opportunity to debrief and to talk through the thinking that took place. In this way, students are able to follow each thread that links the cognitive structures together.

One nursing professor especially likes to use a patient case study as a ticket to class: students have researched the patient case scenario prior to the class session. During the classroom session the students discuss the case in small clinical-based groups, followed by a wrap-up dialogue within the full class with the instructor as discussion facilitator. With this method, students study the factual information from the textbook, as well as the instructor's Power-Point® presentation, and have three separate opportunities to delve into the patient case scenario (S.E. Miller, personal communication, July 1, 2019).

Another complement to the traditional lecture is providing voice-over to the classroom slides for students to be able to replay and study in their own time (C. Morgan, personal communication, June 18, 2019). In this way, students are able to review important points, and it allows more in-class time for guided activities.

In order to foster sound clinical judgment, faculty are using focused contextual clinical assignments rather than the traditional skill repetition models (Nielsen, 2009). Skill repetition is still vitally important, but critical thinking skills transcend time and place and can be applied for the duration of the students' careers. In this way, the clinical instructor can focus students' attention to specific level problem-solving on a given day in the clinic/hospital setting. The instructor can more effectively assist the student in building the constructs of developing sound, timeless critical thinking, and clinical judgment.

IMPLEMENTATION OF CONCEPTUAL TEACHING

Old habits are not easily changed. Teaching the way that faculty were taught is a default setting. As the 21st century rapidly moves forward, paradigm shifts will be occurring in technology, industry, and global culture, and education will shift in order to remain relevant. As with many changes, a dramatic pendulum swing occurs at first, followed by a leveling out in both philosophy and practice.

This leveling out will need to see changes to higher education, in methodology as well as in outcomes. Faculty will be able to sift through passing fads and begin to connect the most appropriate and effective contemporary teaching methods with the desired learning outcomes for their students.

Implementation in K–12 Classrooms

Primary and secondary education settings have implemented many elements of revival that have included teaching conceptually as well as active learning strategies. They have incorporated these newer methods from ongoing professional development as expectations of their practice. Changes to content as well as methodology generally take place at the state and regional levels, rather than at an individual faculty member's discretion. At the local level, faculty plan in groups so that there is consistency in their lessons (C. K. Smith, personal communication, June 22, 2019).

Implementation in Higher Education

For higher education, transitioning from traditional teaching and learning theories has come a bit slower. Many educators in higher education teach as they were taught and govern themselves as to how they choose to teach their content. Academic freedom is a closely guarded attribute of teaching in a college or university. Curriculum changes may occur, but the true transition takes much longer and "those individuals affected by that change will transition at his or her own pace . . . accept[ing] the losses of the past and be[ing] ready to move on and embrace the new" (Deane, 2017, p. 237).

Making Curriculum Changes

Making a curriculum change requires additional work of faculty. "Teaching conceptually may be unfamiliar to faculty, requiring them to develop new pedagogies to promote learning. Transitioning to concept-based teaching may be a challenge to faculty who have a comfort level in their approach to teaching" (Deane, 2017, p. 238). Some faculty may feel that traditional teaching methods are acceptable and that concept-based teaching is not substantially different, or that there is not enough clear direction on how to make the change effectively (M. Casey, L. Galloway, personal communication, June 17, 2019).

The employing colleges or universities would do well to enable a lighter workload, if possible, during the planning stages of a curriculum design change. A supportive administration will help to recognize and alleviate concerns that faculty will have, such as "fear of failure, giving up power, loss of uniqueness, and a potential for a decline in student success" (Deane, 2017, p. 239). Additionally, Howser and Schwinn (1997) offer:

> Some guiding principles and philosophies for educators planning to move toward the new paradigm of learning include the following:
> 1. Keep the focus
> 2. Expect conflict, unhappiness, and pain
> 3. Be open to honest criticism
> 4. Involve everyone
> 5. Promote constant communication
> 6. Double your time estimates
> 7. Provide coping strategies
> 8. Provide for 'new' learning
> 9. Use specialized language sparingly
> 10. People will react differently
> 11. Control rumors. (pp. 146–147).

One study of nursing faculty who had undergone a concept-based curriculum change to their program revealed several factors which were helpful to them in managing the transition including, "identifying inner support, building team cohesiveness, learning from and sharing knowledge with others, and seeing positive student outcomes" (Deane, 2017, p. 239). Remaining positive and open with an inquisitive mindset appears to be the best way to approach such potentially dramatic changes. Realizing that teaching is also a learning process is critical and that "if we are not 'coach-able,' the learning process is far more difficult and slower than it needs to be" (Erickson & Lanning, 2014, p. 53).

The Students

What about the students? Students learn differently from one another and some are very receptive to a more inquisitive, participative method of instruction, while others are not. Some students do not care for group activities, although collaborative learning can be very effective and beneficial for students (Graham, 1996). Some students remark that they feel that they are having to teach themselves (S.E. Miller, personal communication, July 1, 2019). Others are remarkably receptive to the hands-on, active approaches.

Offering a variety of learning opportunities for students, however, allows for various learning styles to be effective. Offering content multicontextually allows learners who prefer differing levels of context to be successful, and can facilitate learning in all students, particularly culturally diverse students who may have culturally impacted learning styles (Giddens et al., 2008). In other words, students from various backgrounds may learn better from higher or lower context teaching strategies. A lower context lesson, such as a factual lecture or reading would appeal to some, while a higher context lesson, such as a realistic clinical simulation would fit still other learning styles better.

LOOKING TO THE FUTURE

The future will bring about significant changes in higher education. The students coming to community colleges and universities are digital natives and are quite comfortable and used to learning with and from technology. They are used to accessing bits of information as they need it for the task at hand. To learn a new discipline, course, or technical trade, the education must meet them where they are. This is the hallmark of adult education.

Vast Amounts of Knowledge

It stands to reason that with an ever-changing, complex world, changes in teaching and learning must occur that rise to the occasion. Former instructional methods are out of step with what will be expected of our graduates. As such, our "curricula need to reflect the changes in society and the environment" (Erickson & Lanning, 2014, p. 132). If students know where to locate good, reliable information as well as how to continue life-long learning, higher education will have succeeded in its quest.

Program Length

The length of curriculum programs in higher education will likely remain the same, at least for now. Therefore, students really have to learn more within the same timeframe. There is so much information to learn in any discipline, that teaching conceptually makes sense, if only to be able to instill larger, broader chunks of information into learners. As information outdates, faculty must make decisions as to what stays in the curriculum and what is replaced with more current knowledge (Giddens & Brady, 2007). These decisions are not easy to make, as the education experts deem all information to be vital.

According to Giddens and Brady (2007), "an organizational shift . . . to a conceptual approach requires a complex curriculum design and is a 'quantum leap' for faculty" (p. 67), who are used to teaching in a factual, linear, repetitious fashion. Teaching conceptually can allow for less repetition, although students should have opportunities to practice and repeat skills as needed, perhaps outside of class.

Outcomes of Conceptual Learning

A number of positive outcomes from conceptual teaching and learning have emerged, including "enhanced synthesis, reasoning, and analysis skills; improved problem-solving skills; ability to translate theory to practice; appreciation of linear and nonlinear ways of thinking; and enhanced concept construction" (Fletcher et al., 2019, p. 13). It stands to reason that the higher level of thinking that will be required of 21st-century graduates will demand a curriculum that embeds high-level, conceptual knowledge.

Learners are more engaged with content to which they have a vivid connection. They are able to integrate knowledge more quickly and assimilate it into their lives and problem-solving domain. They can recognize patterns and links readily (Fletcher et al., 2019). In fact:

> Concept-based learning is intellectually and emotionally engaging for students. Because teachers value student thinking and make it visible in the classroom, there is an excitement—an intellectual buzz that permeates the room. Students realize it is okay to make mistakes because that is how we all learn. Nothing motivates students more for success than feeling they are important members of the classroom learning community and being recognized for using their minds and working hard in collaboration with others. Concept-based curriculum, instruction, and learning are the threads that are woven smoothly in to create an educational tapestry that values each student as a person, a thinker, and a learner (Erickson & Lanning, 2014, p. 131).

Conceptual learning is truly a different way of presenting and processing information.

Higher education attempts to prepare graduates for the workforce, especially in community colleges. Concept-based curricula are aimed not only at higher-level thinking but also at preparing students to think through real-life situations and to be *job-ready*. They will already be used to thinking like someone who works in the field, rather than someone who has the *book-knowledge,* but no ability to apply principles practically. According to

Giddens and Brady (2007), "a concept-based curriculum coupled with a conceptual learning approach can prepare graduates who are skilled at conceptual thinking and learning; such skills are necessary to respond to a rapidly changing profession and healthcare environment" (p. 68).

CONCLUSION

The 21st century is here. When educators are ready to revisit and revise how they construct their curricula, as well as how to promote student success in the digital age, they will certainly consider conceptual teaching and learning. Faculty can delve into curricular resources related to conceptual approaches for the benefit of their students. The conceptual learning classroom will successfully integrate lower- and higher-level reasoning to bridge factual with conceptual thinking (Erickson et al., 2017). This level of thinking will enable the 21st-century graduates to process information and rapid change more quickly and efficiently. They will be ready.

CHAPTER SUMMARY

- College professors have had the reputation having a teaching philosophy of *if I don't say it, they can't learn it.*
- Concept-based curricula are not new to education, but not widely used in postsecondary settings.
- Concept-based education has its roots in constructivist learning theory in that both view context as an enhancement to the learning process.
- With the constructivist approach, students are active, with both mental and psychomotor skills.
- Learners form linkages from the new information to previously learned concepts.
- Conceptual learning leads the instructor to use methods that fosters a deep level of learning rather than memorization of facts for exams.
- Conceptual learning can help students think critically.
- In healthcare, graduates need to continually evolve and add to their knowledge.
- Since conceptual learning is an active learning style, educators must use active learning strategies.
- Conceptual teaching allows the student to see the facts and skills learned to come alive in real situations.
- Students learn to apply facts to broader, overarching concepts.

- Guiding questions help the learner to move through both facts and concepts related to the content.
- One area of trepidation for educators is that teaching conceptually may overlook the facts in a discipline.
- Very young children can learn from each other and begin to see relationships within the concepts they study.
- Older elementary-aged children might study the concept of change through a problem-solving learning activity.
- At the high school level, teachers can organize content around a vision or big idea.
- The teacher of literature could use the short story, novel, or poem as vehicles for learning concepts.
- Bringing real-life context to learning activities can increase the conceptual processing and application.
- When teaching adult basic education, it is important to conceptualize learning into something that is relevant to the adult student.
- Health science disciplines have struggled with content saturation.
- Nursing has been at the forefront of recent progress with concept-based higher education.
- In order to foster sound clinical judgment, faculty are using focused contextual clinical assignments rather than traditional repetition models.
- Teaching the way the faculty were taught is a default setting.
- Making a curriculum change requires additional work of faculty.
- College and universities would do well to create of lighter teaching load during the planning stages of curriculum design change.
- Realizing that teaching is also a learning process is critical to keep in mind.
- Offering a variety of learning opportunities for students allows for various learning styles to be effective.
- Students coming to community colleges and universities are used to learning from technology.
- Former instructional methods are out of step with what will be expected of graduates.
- As information outdates, faculty must make decisions as to what remains in the curriculum and what is replaced.
- Teaching conceptually can allow for less repetition.
- Concept-based curricula are aimed not only at higher-level thinking but also at preparing students to think through real-life situations and to be job-ready.
- Conceptual learning will enable 21st-century students to process information and rapid change more quickly and efficiently.

NOTE

1. Editor's Note: This chapter delves into the process of moving education from the faculty member's position of the sage-on-the-stage to that of focusing on student learning through the understanding of concepts with the faculty member as the guide on the side.

Education is not the learning of facts, but the training of the mind to think.
—Albert Einstein

REFERENCES

Deane, W. H. (2017). Transitioning to concept-based teaching: A qualitative descriptive study from the nurse educator's perspective. *Teaching and Learning in Nursing, 12*(4), 237–241. doi: 10.1016/j.teln.2017.06.006.

Erickson, H. L. (2002). *Concept-based curriculum and instruction: Teaching beyond the facts.* Thousand Oaks, CA: Corwin Press.

Erickson, H. L., & Lanning, L. A. (2014). *Transitioning to concept-based curriculum and instruction: How to bring content and process together.* Thousand Oaks, CA: Corwin Press.

Erickson, H. L., Lanning, L. A., & French, R. (2017). *Concept-based curriculum and instruction for the thinking classroom* (2nd ed.). Thousand Oaks, CA: Corwin Press.

Fletcher, K. A., Hicks, V. L., Johnson, R. H., Laverentz, D. M., Phillips, C. J., Pierce, L. N. B., Wilhoite, D. L. & Gay, J. E. (2019). A concept analysis of conceptual learning: A guide for educators. *Journal of Nursing Education, 58*(1), 7–15.

Giddens, J. F., & Brady, D. P. (2007). Rescuing nursing education from content saturation: The case for a concept-based curriculum. *Journal of Nursing Education, 46*(2), 65–69.

Giddens, J. F., Brady, D. P., Brown, P., Wright, M., Smith, D., & Harris, J. (2008). A new curriculum for a new era of nursing education. *Nursing Education Perspectives, 29*(4), 200–204.

Giddens, J. F., Caputi, L., & Rodgers, B. (2015). *Mastering concept-based teaching: A guide for nurse educators.* St. Louis, MO: Elsevier.

Graham, C. L. (1996). Conceptual learning processes in physical therapy students. *Physical Therapy, 76*(8), 856–865.

Juvova, A., Chudy, S., Neumeister, P., Plischke, J., & Kvintova, J. (2015). Reflection of constructivist theories in current educational practice. *Universal Journal of Educational Research, 3*(5), 345–349. doi: 10.13189/ujer.2015.030506.

Nielsen, A. (2009). Concept-based learning activities using he clinical judgment model as a foundation for clinical learning. *Journal of Nursing Education, 48*(6), 350–354.

O'Banion, T. (1997). *A learning college for the 21st century.* Phoenix, AZ: The Oryx Press.

Schill, B., & Howell, L. (2011). Concept-based learning. *Science and Children, 48*(6), 40–45.

Smith, R. O. (2014). Beyond passive learning: Problem-based learning and concept maps to promote basic and higher-order thinking in basic skills instruction. *Journal of Research and Practice for Adult Literacy, Secondary, and Basic Education, 3*(2), 50–55.

Chapter 2

Project-Based Education[1]

Maria Williams

In the 21st-century classroom students need certain skills to be prepared for academics, their chosen career paths, and the responsibilities of life in general. A primary purpose of education is to help students be better learners and better workers. It is important that students acquire and cultivate transferable skills such as communication, problem-solving, and teamwork. Project-based learning can provide learners with the opportunity to develop these skills. The method will also challenge students to be adaptable, flexible thinkers.

WHAT IS PROJECT-BASED LEARNING?

Project-based learning (PBL) is a student-driven, teacher-facilitated approach to learning (Bell, 2010). This learning approach is not a new method, but is an emerging perspective due to the critical 21st-century skills that are needed and cultivated. No matter the learner's education level, the learning approach will be able to engage all. PBL encourages learners to be self-directing; therefore, learning outcomes depend on the ability and proclivity for a topic or problem and peer collaboration. PBL is learner-centered instruction that places the student at the center of learning.

There is no precise way to define PBL. The main premise of the instructional method is problem-solving. Learners pursue knowledge by asking questions that have piqued their natural curiosity (Bell, 2010). The initial stage of a project is an inquiry (Bell, 2010). The method provides students with opportunities to help choose the project, study a challenging problem, engage in sustained inquiry, find answers to authentic questions, reflect on the process, critique and revise their work, and create a final product.

Cognitive Engagement

PBL fosters cognitive engagement. Larmer, Mergendoller, and Boss (2015) suggest that PBL is a powerful teaching method that motivates students; prepares students for college, career, and citizenship; and helps students to demonstrate in-depth knowledge and thinking skills. There are criteria that must be fulfilled for a project to be meaningful. According to Larmer and Mergendoller (2010), a project is meaningful, if first, the students perceive it as personally meaningful. Second, a meaningful project fulfills an educational purpose. A well-designed and well-implemented PBL project is meaningful in both ways (Larmer & Mergendoller, 2010).

PBL aims to develop self-regulated learning within students (Hunter-Doniger, 2018). As opposed to traditional, instructor-centered instruction, students learn how and where to find information as well as how to apply it to formulate an answer or solution of their own. As students become active participants in the learning process, expand their content knowledge and material usage (Hunter-Doniger, 2018).

Essential Components

Larmer and Mergendoller (2010) suggests that there are eight essential components that must be present to effectively implement and carry out PBL: significant content, a need to know, a driving question, student choice, 21st-century competencies, in-depth inquiry, critique and revision, and a publicly presented product. Significant content entails teachers planning student work around important content will allow students to understand a topic even more (Larmer & Mergendoller, 2010).

Teachers should plan a project to focus on important knowledge and content standards. The content should reflect what the teachers thinks is essential to understanding the topic the project is going to cover. Students should find the content to be significant in terms of their own lives and interests (Larmer & Mergendoller, 2010).

A need to know entails students finding purpose in their work. Many students find schoolwork meaningless because they do not perceive that they need to know what is being taught. Teachers should powerfully activate students' need to know content by launching a project with an entry event that engages student interests and initiates questioning (Larmer & Mergendoller, 2010).

An entry event can be anything that will engage students: a video, discussion, guest speaker, a field trip, or piece of mock correspondence that sets up a scenario. A compelling student project will display to students that the information being learned is relevant, there it becomes clear and students are engaged (Larmer & Mergendoller, 2010).

Driving Question

A driving question entails the teachers guiding students in clarifying the point of a project. According to Larmer and Mergendoller (2010), a driving question captures the heart of the project in clear, compelling language that gives student a sense of purpose and challenge. The driving question should be provocative, open-ended, complex, and linked to the core of what teachers want students to learn. A driving question can be abstract or concrete, but focus must be on solving the problem. Without a driving question, students may not clearly understand why they are undertaking a project (Larmer & Mergendoller, 2010).

Student Choice

Student choice is a key component in PBL because more the choices, the better. According to Larmer and Merdendoller (2010), teachers must design projects with the extent of student choice that fits their own learning style. Students should be given the option to choose how to design, create, and present projects. Students can decide what will be created from the project, what resources will be used, and how they will structure their time (Larmer & Mergendoller, 2010).

The development of 21st-century competencies entails students acquiring necessary skills and utilizing technology to be prepared for learning in the 21st century. Collaboration is central to a PBL project and a necessary skill needed. Students should form teams to begin planning what they should do and how they plan to work together. As students work together, they are engaging and communicating (Larmer & Mergendoller, 2010).

According to Larmer and Mergendoller (2010), a project provides students with opportunities to build 21st-century competencies such as critical thinking, collaboration, communication, and creativity/innovation. These competencies will serve them well in the workplace and life. A teacher in the PBL environment explicitly teaches and assesses these skills and provides frequent opportunities for students to assess themselves (Larmer & Mergendoller, 2010).

Research

In-depth inquiry entails students finding project work to be more meaningful because they are tasked with conducting real inquiry. Conducting real inquiry encourages students to be innovative (Larmer & Mergendoller, 2010). As a result, this leads to students developing their own questions, searching for resources and the discovery of answers, generating new questions, testing ideas, and drawing their own conclusions (Larmer & Mergendoller, 2010).

Critique and Revision

Critique and revision entails students reviewing and critiquing one another's work. As students develop their ideas and work to solve a problem, student teams also review and critique one another's work. Students must learn and understand that most initial attempts do not result in high quality and that revision is a consistent feature of real-world work. Teachers must formalize a process for critique and revision during a project because these will ensure that learning become more meaningful for students (Larmer & Mergendoller, 2010).

Public Audience

Public audience or publicly presented product entails students presenting their work to a real audience that has a vested interest in their learning. Schoolwork is more meaningful when it is not only done for teachers or a test, but also done for those that have a vested interest in students' education. When students are provided the opportunities to present their work to a real audience, they will care more about the quality of the work (Larmer & Mergendoller, 2010).

PBL IN K–12 AND HIGHER EDUCATION

PBL as a teaching method in K–12 instruction and higher education is gaining momentum. The teaching method affords students with a learning experience that is authentic with real-world application. Most importantly, it is centered on the student and allows them to direct their learning.

K–12 Education

The K–12 education system is transforming. Educators are seeking innovative and engaging ways to interact with students. The transformation and the exploration of engaging methods to interact with students are confirming that students need to possess well-developed critical thinking, higher-level thinking, collaborative abilities, and real-world skillsets (Grossman, Pupik Dean, Schneider Kavanagh, & Herrman, 2019). Students will be expected to demonstrate their ability to think and reason when problem-solving

(Larmer et al., 2015). PBL can assist students with developing and cultivating the necessary skills.

Developing Independent Thinking

PBL helps teachers establish classrooms that produce independent thinkers and learners (Grossman et al., 2019). PBL shifts student thinking. The teaching method literally captivates students. Students solve real-world problems by designing their own inquiries or investigations, planning their learning, organizing their research, and implementing a variety of learning strategies (Bell, 2010). As PBL is implemented into content and daily instruction, students flourish under this student-driven, motivating approach to learning and gain valuable skills that build a strong foundation for college and career-readiness (Buck Institute for Education, 2013).

PBL is not simply "doing a project." It is important that teachers differentiate this when students are learning to research and evaluate material. Students are learning to be autonomous and manage their own learning. Teachers must establish timeframes that connect projects of meaning with standards-based teaching (Bell, 2010). The Buck Institute for Education (BIE) is an organization that has completed extensive research and is the primary resource for information on PBL (Larmer et al., 2015).

The organization defines PBL as "a standards-focused systematic teaching method that engages students in learning knowledge and skills through an extended inquiry process structured around complex, authentic questions and carefully designed products and tasks" (Buck Institute for Education, 2013). It is important to note that the complexity of the content being explored and the driving questions for projects will be determined by the age and grade-level of the students (Thomas, 2000).

Students' Individual Learning Style

PBL is inclusive and equalizes the learning process (Bell, 2010). The method respects and reflects students' individual learning style and emphasizes the learning process guided by each individual learner (Buck Institute for Education, 2013). PBL has the potential to take on various formats and definitions. The BIE model focuses on standards, content, accountability, and performance, and it narrows the gap between the expectations of the education system and the ideals of sound educational theory. BIE states that a "standards-focused, systematic teaching method" indicates a well-planned, well-organized teaching and learning process (Buck Institute for Education, 2013).

Essential Elements

As mentioned, there are essential elements that are fundamental to PBL: significant content, students' need to know, driving question, student voice and choice, develop 21st-century skills, in-depth inquiry or inquiry innovation, critique or feedback and revision, and publicly presented product/audience (Larmer & Mergendoller, 2010).

In addition to ensuring that the fundamental steps are included in instruction, teachers must also outline the direction of a project for students. BIE (2013) suggests four key steps teachers can utilize to put students on the right path: organizing tasks and activities, deciding how to launch the project, gathering resources, and drawing a storyboard. Organizing tasks and activities entails evaluating student's abilities and individual learning styles, preparing the framework for learning, itemizing tasks, and analyzing the learning outcome(s) (Buck Institute for Education, 2013).

Deciding how to launch a project entails ensuring that the project encompasses mandated state content standards and determining the entry activity for the project (Grossman et al., 2019). Teachers must be creative when identifying an entry activity. The entry activity can be a video, a discussion, a demonstration, or any experiential learning opportunity that engages students (Bell, 2010).

Resources Needed

Gathering resources for the project entails teachers determining what technological tools students will utilize for the projects. In this step, teachers will identify books and community resources relevant to the project and utilize the Internet to identify websites relevant to the project (Larmer et al., 2015). Teachers will ensure that students have necessary supplies such as notebooks, display boards, writing utensils, and paper (www.shsu.edu).

It is important to note that teachers should use resources that will make projects more efficient, and make sure projects have scope and complexity that fosters students' opportunities for investigation (www.shsu.edu). Drawing a storyboard entails the instructor illustrating to students the expectations and progression of a project. A storyboard is a pictorial representation of the developments of a project (Buck Institute for Education, 2013).

Teachers as Managers

It is important that teachers maintain their role as planners and managers of projects. With these responsibilities, they must consider timing and be prepared for unexpected delays in the timing of certain aspects of a project. Aligning the project with content standards will ensure students' understanding of material they will be held accountable for (Bell, 2010). Projects that are inclusive of multiple content areas may take more time but allow for more creativity and exploration (Buck Institute for Education, 2013). Once the process of a project is mastered, PBL has the potential to be a very rewarding learning experience for all involved.

HIGHER EDUCATION

Learning is a building process. When students pursue postsecondary education, they build upon the knowledge that has been bestowed upon them on the secondary level of education. Therefore, in higher education, students are emerging unto the next platform of learning. Postsecondary institutions can implement a PBL curriculum to motivate students to learn on a higher educational level.

Open-Learning Environment

PBL is a creative teaching discipline that helps students develop a global learning perspective (Larmer et al., 2015). The teaching method also establishes an open-learning environment that facilitates career-readiness and encompasses the work community (Larmer et al., 2015). Lifelong learning is the ultimate goal of postsecondary education. PBL implements technology combined with advanced instructional technologies and communicates the need for more inclusiveness for diverse learners (Grossman et al., 2019).

In postsecondary education, student competencies are expected to go beyond just content knowledge and understanding. Students have to be able to apply the content they are learning to their personal lives, and their chosen career path. Instructors have the responsibility of preparing and challenging students to direct their own learning and solve problems of academic significance.

Higher education instructors that implement PBL facilitate learning that moves beyond an environment that fosters controlled information containment. They foster learning environments where ideas are developed, explored, integrated, and resolved with the context of an assignment or area of study. Rather than being the main source of instruction of a subject or area of study, instructors serve as facilitators of knowledge and motivators of active learning (Larmer et al., 2015).

Higher-Level Thinking

The pursuit of higher education requires a higher level of thinking. Higher-level thinking is when students learn to simulate real-world experiences and life-skill expertise (Larmer et al., 2015). PBL encompasses real-work implementation and life-skill acquisition and expertise (Larmer et al., 2015).

PBL can be a motivating factor for students who are not academically successful (Larmer et al., 2015). The teaching method cultivates a learning environment that encourages students to engage and display their learning capabilities. At the postsecondary level, students experience responsibility for academic learning that guides them into the essentials of lifelong learning and are validated through their decisions and actions (Larmer et al., 2015).

PBL implemented within a higher education curriculum promotes learning that is centered on projects or complex tasks that explore an in-depth question or problem. Students are encouraged to be self-directing. The learning path becomes the curriculum as exploration and idea development connects to intended and desired learning outcomes (Larmer et al., 2015).

Initiating PBL

When beginning PBL, instructors often challenge students to start a project with the end in mind (Larmer & Mergendoller, 2010). Topics often start out broad and then narrow as students explore the material and research and discover unknown information that enhances current knowledge (Bell, 2010). The scope of the PBL is larger and broader than a traditional assignment. Application can potentially range from days spent on a project to encompassing the entire semester (Larmer et al., 2015). This is determined by instructors and the desired learning outcomes that have been established.

As with K–12 instruction, PBL in higher education must also incorporate the eight essential elements: significant content, need to know, driving question, voice and choice, 21st-century skills, inquiry and innovation, critique and revision, and a publicly presented product. PBL in higher education assists instructors in motivating students and facilitates new learning relationships. The ultimate goal is to develop lifelong learners with advanced critical thinking skills, good problem-solving skills, active listening skills, and public speaking skills. These career-readiness skills will prepare students for workplace responsibilities and opportunities.

WHERE AND HOW PBL IS ALREADY WORKING SUCCESSFULLY

PBL is not a new teaching method, but as educators explore innovative ways to engage students and ensure that they are prepared the 21st-century workforce, the approach is being implemented and studied on the secondary and postsecondary levels of instruction.

The student-centered teaching method is viewed as a mechanism to deliver academic content in a more engaging way for students and fosters the development of necessary skills such as critical thinking, problem-solving, active listening, collaboration, communication, and public speaking (Bell, 2010). The development of these necessary skills will not only produce well-rounded students that are academically prepared but will also produce students that are prepare for workplace responsibilities and opportunities (Larmer et al., 2015).

K–12

PBL is successfully working in secondary education systems throughout the United States. The New Tech Network (NTN) organization has successfully implemented PBL in over 200 schools and in 28 states. The (NTN) design model is an approach that reimagines the way teaching and learning has previously prepared students for academics and the workforce.

The NTN method strives to deliver instruction that is centered on what the BIE has defined as "Gold Standard PBL." "Gold Standard PBL" defines PBL by student-learning goals, essential project design elements, and PBL teaching practices. The standard stresses that PBL should develop key knowledge and understanding of academic curricula in students while cultivating career-readiness skills (Buck Institute for Education, 2013).

NTN Case Study

A 2013 case study of one NTN school suggested that the application of PBL created an instructional environment that positively impacted student learning, relationships, and technology use and appeared to improve student self-efficacy (Lynch et al., 2013). Academic achievement and college and career-readiness outcomes were analyzed between 2015 and 2017.

The study concluded that NTN ninth graders outperformed demographically similar control students in mathematics and English Language Arts assessments and that there were null findings on some outcomes. NTN eleventh graders outperformed control students on ACT composite scores and on workforce skills outcomes measured by ACT WorkKeys (Culclasure,

Odell, & Stocks, 2017). The 2018 internal NTN Report on School and Student Success reported a 94% high school graduation rate among NTN schools with an 83% persistence rate in college of NTN graduates at two- and four-year institutions (www.newtechnetwork.org).

Higher Education

Higher education institutions have the responsibility of building upon the knowledge that students learned in high school. In addition, they have the responsibility of preparing students for their chosen career paths. Some institutions have successfully integrated the PBL method into curricula or specific areas of program study. One is the Riley Institute at Furman University in Greenville, South Carolina (www.furman.edu).

The Riley Institute

The Riley Institute partnered with the South Carolina Department of Education along with other institutions of higher education that include Furman University, Claflin University, College of Charleston, and Winthrop University, to develop a three-course PBL endorsement for South Carolina's educators. The endorsement not only teaches educators on how to integrate PBL in the classroom to align with content standards, the PBL model is immersed in instruction (Culclasure, B., personal communication, June 7, 2019).

The endorsement integrates PBL methodologies that include the development of projects, analysis of student data, and reflection upon the project development experience. The endorsement is broken down into three-course areas of focus concerning PBL entails driving questions, learning objectives, and key assessments (www.furman.edu).

Course One

Course one is *The Introduction to Project-Based Learning*. The course is designed to introduce students to the theory behind PBL and the basics of designing, delivering, and assessing PBL that supports student attainment of core academic content and such 21st-century skills as personal agency, critical and analytical thinking, collaboration, communication and technological proficiency (www.furman.edu). The driving questions of course one seeks to explore how does PBL changes the dynamics of a classroom and how PBL supports the college and career-readiness vision outlined by the Profile of a South Carolina Graduate?

The learning objectives of course one include identifying characteristics and attributes of PBL, discussing the theories and data to support PBL, comprehending and explaining how PBL supports attainment of content knowledge and college and career skills, comprehending and explaining the advantages and disadvantages of PBL and its implications for student achievement (www.furman.edu).

Course Two

Course two is the *Applications of Project-Based Learning*. The course is a hybrid, classroom and field-based course designed to give teachers the experiences required to plan, create, facilitate, and integrate appropriate instructional methodologies and technology within a PBL unit of study that will support the academic achievement of students with diverse learning needs (www.furman.edu).

Teachers utilize the content knowledge and experiences from course one, design and implement PBL strategies and a project. The driving questions for course two seek to explore what is needed in order to successfully implement a PBL unit, and what do students need to be successful with engaging effectively in PBL (www.furman.edu)?

The learning objectives of course two include demonstrating an understanding of the connections between and among disciplines by constructing PBL units of study that appropriately integrate methods and activities across curriculum standards to facilitate student academic achievement; utilizing community partners, parents, and businesses in the development and implementation of authentic, contextually appropriate PBL units of study; and developing and implementing effective formative and summative assessment instruments for a PBL unit (www.furman.edu).

Course Three

Course three is the *Practicum in Project-Based Learning*. The course is a field-based practicum designed to provide educators with experience and opportunities to demonstrate their knowledge, skills, and dispositions for implementing PBL into the regular classroom setting. This knowledge is demonstrated through planning for, implementing, and managing standards-based PBL and content instruction using a wide range of resources and technology effectively. The instruction is based on the use and interpretation of performance-based assessment tools and PBL techniques (www.furman.edu).

The driving questions of course three explore how can educators build a culture of collaboration in the classroom using PBL, and how educators can become a reflective PBL practitioner.

The learning objectives of the course include developing and implementing PBL unit(s), which may include project description(s), timeline(s), standards-based learning objectives, project rationales, integrative activities, formative and summative assessments, related resources and technological supports, designing and delivering PBL instruction that meets the academic needs of all students, and developing and presenting a professional development introduction to PBL for their peers that could include a grade-level workshop, a department-level workshop, or a school-wide faculty meeting (www.furman.edu).

PBL Endorsement

The PBL endorsement successfully produces teachers that are committed to students and their learning and striving to improve their instructional practices and more effectively engage students in their learning (Culclasure, B. personal communication, June 7, 2019). Teachers can implement well-planned, content-appropriate curriculum and instruction with technology (www.furman.edu).

For example, after successfully completing the PBL endorsement, a Greenville County high school teacher was able to successfully place PBL into her curriculum (www.furman.edu). She successfully used PBL to conduct eco-preneurship contests in her environmental studies classes. Students wrote green business plans for local companies and received weekly mentoring from community members through Facetime and Skype. As a result, students were more interested in the content that was being taught and saw the relevance in what they were learning (www.furman.edu).

IMPLEMENTATION OF PBL IN HIGHER EDUCATION

Higher education has lagged behind K–12 in adopting and integrating PBL into curricula (Lee, Blackwell, Drake, & Moran, 2014). Although many institutions have implemented collaborative and innovative approaches to teaching and learning over the past twenty years, many remain bounded by the lecture/discussion model that is instructor-centered (Lee et al., 2014). It is important that higher education institutions prepare for 21st-century technologies by implementing PBL.

Practical Framework

The practical framework of PBL is continuously emerging as a teaching and learning approach in secondary schools across the America (Rice & Shannon, 2016). Eventually, those students will be expected to learn through this same method of instruction in higher education. PBL demonstrates how instructors can meaningfully integrate 21st-century technologies into classrooms.

As students carry out a content-driven PBL, they will utilize appropriate 21st-century technologies (Rice & Shannon, 2016).

Challenges

Transforming instruction within higher education may prove to be challenging, but student engagement and interaction are important premises of PBL as it will facilitate opportunities to promote collaboration. Projects must be grounded in the real world and focused on meaningful student-learning outcomes (Lee et al., 2014). As a result, students will be motivated and empowered in their learning.

Faculty

To successfully implement PBL into higher education instruction, it is important that faculty recognize the method as a teaching/learning approach that engages students in self-directed learning and incorporates real-work experiences and work to ensure the authenticity of a project (Lee et al., 2014). Faculty must also possess complete understanding of what PBJ is and how the method can effectively and efficiently teach students. Possessing background information of the approach will assist instructors in effectively implementing PBL in instruction. Faculty will also need extensive training on how to implement a successful project into instruction.

To effectively implement PBL in higher education, faculty must be not only aware of the benefits of PBL, but also challenges that may occur. One challenge that faculty may encounter when implementing PBL in higher education is aligning projects with real work (Lee et al., 2014). Some faculty may struggle with identifying what needs to be explored in terms of a project (Lee et al., 2014).

A second challenge faculty may encounter is aligning the project with course objectives and establishing an appropriate timeline for project completion (Lee et al., 2014). A third challenge faculty may face is maintaining the authenticity of project while maintaining student engagement (Lee et al., 2014). To move beyond challenges, it is important that faculty fully understand and embrace PBL. Faculty will also require ongoing and training and mentoring.

STUDENTS' ATTRACTION TO PBL

Students would be attracted to PBL because the method is a student-centered teaching strategy. Rather than having a learning environment where instructors transfer knowledge through lectures and students are passive listeners, PBL will facilitate an environment where students actively learn because cooperation and collaboration is fostered to increase students' self-directed learning capabilities, social skills, and problem-solving skills (Atay, 2014). Instead of students taking on the role as a receiver of information, they take on the role of the actor that is self-directing in their learning (Atay, 2014).

Real-Life Experiences

PBL allows students to apply and exemplify subject matter content on real-life experiences. This provides for the opportunity for students to communicate, engage, and collaborate with other students (Atay, 2014). This also provides the opportunity for student to reflect where they are learning through the transformation of their experiences (Atay, 2014).

Education theorists have long maintained that educators need to explore more engaging, autonomous, authentic, problem-solving, collaborative methods for teaching and learning (Rice & Shannon, 2016). PBL will challenge students into engaging into these components. The richness of a good project can be beneficial to students because it enhances and promotes a deeper understanding of the material students are exploring (Blumenfeld et al., 1991). Students will acquire and apply information, concepts, and principles and have the potential to improve critical thinking skills (Blumenfeld et al., 1991).

PBL AND 21ST-CENTURY TECHNOLOGIES

As 21st-century technologies impact higher education, business as usual will be redefined. Institutions must be prepared for and able to control the continuous changes the technologies will produce (Staat, 2019). Courses and certificates that reflect the new technologies will be added, programs will be modified, and stackable credentials will become the norm to address the rapidly changing educational environment.

Student and Faculty Needs

With the redefining of business, the needs of students and faculty will change. Students will need to be properly trained to keep up with a business community that is competing globally. Students will need to be workforce members that are well-educated, future focused, and data driven. Faculty and staff will need to be continually re-educated and retrained to adapt to change in individual attitudes, focus, and expertise (Staat, 2019). Institutions of higher education can implement PBJ to address the demand of the 21st-century technologies.

PBL prepares students for working in the 21st-century workforce and for living in the global community (Hunter & Botchwey, 2016). PBL helps instructors to recognize that are certain skills and dispositions needed by students for them to be college and career ready (Hunter & Botchwey, 2016).

Skills Needed

These necessary skills and dispositions are critical thinking skills, analytical thinking skills, problem-solving skills, feedback, possible failures at times, clear and convincing written and oral expression, and use reasoning for weighing importance and credibility of materials. Furthermore, when the business community is consulted on what it takes to succeed in the workplace, in addition job-specific knowledge and skills, a similar list is generated (Lamer et al., 2015).

CONCLUSION

PBL is an effective, innovative student-centered approach to learning. The method teaches students essential skills to ensure that they are college and career ready. Students design projects that reflect real work that is centered around research, reflection, communication, and collaborative. As 21st-century technologies continue to impact higher education, PBL is a learning approach that can be implemented to address the needs of institutions and business community.

CHAPTER SUMMARY

- PBL is a student-driven, teacher-facilitated approach to learning.
- PBL encourages students to be self-directed and aims to develop self-regulated learning within students.
- Teachers using PBL should plan a project to focus on important knowledge and content standards.
- Many students need to know that the information being learned is relevant, which causes the student to get engaged.
- The driving question to be investigated should be provocative, open-ended, complex, and linked to what is needed to be learned.
- Student choice is a key component of PBL because the more choice the better.

- The project itself should develop 21st-century competencies such as critical thinking, collaboration, and creativity/innovation.
- Critique and revision entails students reviewing and critiquing one another's work.
- Public audience entails students presenting their work to a real audience.
- PBL helps teachers to produce independent thinkers and learners.
- Students learn to be autonomous and manage their own learning.
- PBL reflects the student's individual learning style and emphasizes the learning process guided by the individual learner.
- Teachers can use four key steps to assist students: organizing tasks and activities, preparing the framework for learning, itemizing tasks, and analyzing learning outcomes.
- Drawing a story board entails the instructor illustrating to students the expectations and progression of the project.
- Teachers play the role of planners and project managers.
- PBL is a creative teaching discipline that helps the students to develop a global learning perspective that can be a motivating factor for students who are not academically successful.
- PBL in higher education focuses on projects that explore in-depth questions or problems.
- The ultimate goal is to develop lifelong learners with advanced skills.
- The student-centered teaching method delivers academic content in a more engaging way.
- In K–12, the NTN design model reimagines teaching and learning.
- Schools using the NTN reported a 94% high school graduation and an 83% retention rate in higher education.
- The Riley Institute partnered with higher education institutions in South Carolina.
- Specific higher education courses have been developed to foster PBL.
- The successful use of PBL in higher education assists teachers who are committed to students and their learning through instructional practices that engage students effectively.
- The practical framework of PBL is continuously emerging as a teaching and learning approach across America.
- To effectively implement PBL in higher education, faculty must be aware of not only the benefits of PBL, but also the challenges that may occur.
- Faculty may find it difficult to align projects with real work.
- Faculty may find it difficult to complete projects within the semester.
- Students would be attracted to PBL because it is a student-centered learning strategy.
- PBL students apply subject matter to real-life experiences.

- Student using PBL will acquire information and the potential to improve critical thinking skills.
- PBL is a method to prepare students for working in the 21st century and for living in a global community.
- As 21st-century technologies continue to impact higher education, PBL is an approach that can address the needs of the business community.

NOTE

1. Editor's Note: At first glance concept-based education and project-based education may seem similar, in that they both call for a student-focused learning. However, a closer look will reveal two distinct models. Both have their strengths. The subject matter being studied determines which of these two make the most sense to use.

REFERENCES

Altay, B. (2014). User-centered design through learner-centered instruction. *Teaching in Higher Education, 19*(2), 138–155. doi: 10.1080/13562517.2013.827646.

Bell, S. (2010). Project-based learning for the 21st century: Skills for the future. *The Clearing House: A Journal of Educational Strategies, Issue and Ideas, 83*, 39–43. doi: 10.1080/00098650903505415.

Blumenfeld, P. C., Soloway, E., Marx, R. W., Krajcik, J. S., Guzdial, M., & Palinscar, A. (1991). Motivating project-based learning: Sustaining the doing, supporting the learning. *Educational Psychologist, 25*(3&4), 369–398. doi: 10.1080/0046119919653139.

Buck Institute for Education [BIE]. (2013). Project-based learning for the 21st century. Retrieved from http://www.bie.org.

Culclasure, B., Odell, M., & Stocks, E. (2017). *New tech network interim evaluation report: Project years 2013–14, 2014–15, and 2015–16 i3 and expanded evaluation samples*. Greenville, SC: Furman University.

Grossman, P., Pupik Dean, C. G., Schneider Kavanagh, S., & Herrman, Z. (2019). Preparing teachers for project-based teaching. *Phi Delta Kappan, 100*(7), 43–48. Retrieved from https://www.kappanonline.org/.

Hunter, P. E. & Botchwey, N. D. (2016). Partnerships in learning: A collaborative project between higher education students and elementary school students. *Innovative Higher Education, 42*, 77–90. doi: 10.1007/s107550169369x.

Hunter-Doniger, T. (2018). Project-based learning; utilizing artistic pedagogies for educational leadership. *Art Education, 71*(2), 46–51. doi: 10.10880/00043125.2018.1414542.

Larmer, J., & Mergendoller, J. (2010). Buck institute for education. Retrieved from www.bie.org.

Larmer, J., Mergendoller, J., & Boss, S. (2015). Why project-based learning? In *Setting the standard for project-based learning* (pp. 1–23). Alexandria, VA: ASDC.

Lee, J. S., Blackwell, S., Drake, J., & Moran, K. A. (2014). Taking a leap of faith: Redefining teaching and learning in higher education through project-based learning. *Interdisciplinary Journal of Problem-Based Learning, 8*(2), 19–34. doi: 10.7771/154150151426.

Lynch, S., Peters-Burton, E., Spillane, N., Behrend, T., Ross, K., House, A., & Han, E. (2013). *Manor new tech high school: A case study of an inclusive STEM-focused high school in manor*. Texas.

Rice, M., & Shannon, L. (2016). Developing project-based learning, integrated courses form two different at an institution of higher education: An overview of the processes, challenges, and lessons learner. *Information Systems Education Journal, 14*(3), 55–62. Retrieved from https://eric.ed.gov/?id=EJ1136184.

Staat, D. (2019). *Exponential technologies: Higher education in an era of serial disruptions*. Lanham, MD: Rowman and Littlefield.

Thomas, J. (2000). A review of search on project-based learning. Retrieved from www.bobpearlman.org/BestPractices/PBL_Research.pdf.

www.furman.edu.

www.newtechnetwork.edu.

www.shsu.edu/centers/project-based-learning/.

Chapter 3

Online Education[1]

Donald Miller

Online education has now been around long enough to make it clear that it is not going away. Those in the field for some time can remember the days when naysayers could credibly say that online education was a fad that would soon be replaced. It was students who made online education work. They have enjoyed the convenience of working from home. In an increasingly technological world, they have enjoyed a mode that uses the latest advancements.

However, now that online education has grown in popularity, it is time to take a serious look at student success. This chapter endeavors to do just that, along with discussing why students find the mode of online education so appealing. First, the current teaching methods will be looked at in K–12, community colleges, and universities. Next, the chapter will analyze in which cases online education has been the most effective. Finally, it will posit future uses for online education, particularly as they relate to massive technological change.

CURRENT DISTANCE EDUCATION TEACHING METHOD

K–12 Schools

More and more states are giving K–12 students the option of attending online. According to Pazhouh, Lake, and Miller (2015), 27 states had online charter schools in 2015. These schools enrolled approximately 200,000 students in the 2013–14 school year (Pazhouh et al., 2015). Over half of all online charter school students live in three states: Ohio, Pennsylvania, and California (Pazhouh et al., 2015). State by state, online enrollment is frequently concentrated in a few large schools administered by companies like Connections Academy and K12 Inc (Pazhouh et al., 2015).

Benefits

Some of the benefits of online charter schools include the following: students in remote areas might get access to better instruction; students with health problems could still go to school; teachers could teach from home; and teachers would have the ability to personalize material. However, some have been critical of online charter schools. Because for-profit educational companies administer most online charter schools, critics suspect that educational quality is not as important as the financial bottom line. Politicians have raised the concern of evaluation: How can teachers in an online charter school environment be overseen effectively (Pazhouh et al., 2015)?

Critics

Critics are also concerned with how the school's results can be assessed fairly and accurately measuring whether taxpayer money has been spent wisely (Pazhouh et al., 2015). According to Strauss (2015), a report by the Center on Reinventing Public Education (CRPE) indicated that the average student who attends charter schools might as well not enroll. What Strauss (2015) meant is that the study indicated that students lost an average of 180 days of instruction in math, roughly equivalent to an entire school year.

An analysis of K12 Inc. "argued that online charter schools, in their need to capture market share and revenues, have overreached by recruiting students who are not well equipped to succeed in the online environment" (Pazhouh et al., 2015, p. 6). For instance, it is not clear those students with special needs or with limited ability to speak English are sufficiently accommodated in online charter schools. It is also not clear that low-income students have sufficient access to technology to be successful in online charter schools (Pazhouh et al., 2015).

Community Colleges and Universities

The research of Jaggars and Xu (2016) indicated that community colleges have led the way in developing online courses (as cited in Travers, 2016). Cejda (2010) showed that going back to 2006, community colleges enrolled more distance-learning students than did universities (as cited in Travers, 2016). In 2007 it was found that 97% of community colleges were offering distance education courses, which was a far higher amount than the 66% at universities for the same year (Parsad and Lewis (2008) as cited in Travers, 2016).

Travers (2016) believed that considering the student body that community colleges serve, it was no surprise that enrollment in distance educations classes was high. Many community college students have limited access to education; some are adult students who have full-time jobs or are full-time caretakers (Travers, 2016).

Online education classes afford these students the opportunity to take classes they might not otherwise be able to take. "For many nontraditional students wishing to pursue higher education goals, online learning is not only appealing, but *necessary*" (Travers, 2016, p. 50). Additionally, students in rural areas find distance education classes appealing because they gain access to opportunities they might not otherwise have gotten (Travers, 2016).

Use of Learning Management Systems

Online Education programs typically use a learning management system (LMS) to teach their courses. Popular LMSs include Blackboard, Moodle, and Canvas. Each of these LMS have discussion forums, the ability to turn assignments in on line, the ability for instructors to post resources like notes, PowerPoints, and videos and the ability to link to resources that the student might find helpful. It is widely agreed that student engagement is very important for online courses. Generally, students who are engaged, do well, while those who are not, do poorly.

Engagement Issues

The problem is that many students are disengaged. This could be a result of an instructor not communicating clear instructions, not being present in the class, or not effectively using the tools provided through the LMS. Alternatively, the disengagement could be the fault of the student. Perhaps, the student does not manage his/her time effectively or is not motivated and self-directed enough to be successful in an online class.

Vice president of Technology Services at Surry Community College in North Carolina Candace Holder sees student disengagement as one of the biggest problems in online courses (C. Holder, personal communication, July 12, 2019). There are several organizations that advise instructors on best practices for teaching online classes; two of the most respected are Quality Matters and The Online Learning Consortium's Quality Framework.

Quality Matters Standards

Quality Matters provides professional development: a rubric that colleges can use to evaluate online courses, and a contracted review service. Quality

Matters' peer-review rubric is guided by several course standards. These include that the student fully understands the design of the course at the outset of the semester and that the objectives of the course are clearly explained. These objectives should help the students know how to focus time spent on the course (qualitymatters.org, 2016).

Another objective is that the course has effective assessments that clearly align with learning objectives. Next, there are enough resources provided to the student, so that he/she can meet the course objectives. The design of the course should allow for multiple ways for the instructor to interact with students and for students to interact with fellow students. Next, the course uses technology to engage students and provides the same support services students in a face-to-face class would get (qualitymatters.org, 2016).

Finally, the course is accessible to all students (qualitymatters.org, 2016). These guidelines give a course builder a good idea of what should be included in a successful course: clear expectations, frequent communication, engaging course materials and assignments, accessibility, and use of technology that enhances learning. Holder said instruments like Quality Matters are necessary because course subjects are taught online now that would not have been considered 10–15 years ago (C. Holder, personal communication, July 12, 2019).

The Online Learning Consortium

The Online Learning Consortium holds a national conference, provides resources and consultations, and gives colleges a peer-review instrument to use (Online Learning Consortium, 2019). The Online Learning Consortium provides a point-based scorecard that can be used to evaluate online courses.

Scorecard

The scorecard used by the Online Learning Consortium assigns points for how effectively the course clarifies and meets course outcomes and course content, whether assignments are clearly connected to course objectives, whether the instructor is an active presence in the course, whether the course discussions engage students, whether the course builds community among students, how effectively the instructor communicates with students, and whether the course is effectively evaluated and improved (Online Learning Consortium, 2016).

The consortium's standards echo those of Quality Matters in that there are clear course outcomes, that the instructor regularly communicates and engages with students, and that technology is used to enhance, rather than hinder, course content.

WHERE AND HOW THE TEACHING METHOD IS ALREADY WORKING

K–12 Schools

Distance education provides educational opportunities for students who might not normally have them. One example is Advanced Placement (AP) classes. From 2002–2012, the number of students who took AP classes doubled (Gagnon & Mattingly, 2016). However, a 2004 study conducted by Klopfenstein indicated rural counties were less likely to offer AP classes (as cited in Gagnon & Mattingly, 2016).

Gagnon and Mattingly (2016) found that only 51.4% of rural school districts offered AP classes, while 93.8% of suburban and 97.3% of urban districts offered the same classes. Barnard-Brak et al. (2011) found that school districts with high minority populations were less likely to participate in AP (as cited in Fenty & Allio, 2017). Researchers found that among minority groups, African American students were the least likely to enroll in AP classes (Fenty & Allio, 2017).

Lack of Access

This lack of access is important because multiple studies indicate that participation in AP classes indicate future success in college classes (Gagnon & Mattingly, 2016). "In districts without AP access, even the most gifted students might not have the opportunity to earn college credit in high school, and could face a disadvantage in applying to elite colleges" (Gagnon and Mattingly, p. 268). Gifted students could be at a disadvantage if they did not have the opportunity to take AP classes. Many universities weigh success in AP classes are part of their admissions standards; students who take no AP classes could be at a disadvantage as compared to their peers.

One solution to this lack of access is Virtual AP, which is offered in 28 states (Gagnon & Mattingly, 2016). According to Gagnon and Mattingly (2016), this option "is especially attractive in hard-to-staff subject areas" (p. 280). It was found that students enrolled in an online high school in Florida did better than students enrolled in face-to-face high school (Johnston and Barbour (2013) as cited by Fenty & Allio, 2017). According to Fenty and Allio (2017), "enrollment in a distance AP program may not compromise the quality of the content provided to the students" (p. 43). If this is the case, distance learning can provide a wonderful opportunity for minority and rural students.

Governmental Regulations

As government regulations on accessibility have tightened, online courses have become more of an attractive option for students with disabilities. According to Smith and Basham (2014), online courses are increasingly "a viable option" for students with disabilities. Universal Design for Learning (UDL) is a framework used by teachers to determine whether their courses are accessible (Smith & Basham, 2014).

Tenets of UDL include that the student has various ways of engaging with the instructor and his peers, that the student has multiple ways of accessing course materials, and that the student has multiple ways of demonstrating their understanding of material (Smith & Basham, 2014). However, since many K–12 online schools are run by large, corporate entities, it can be difficult to "determine if a content developer that features video and explicit instruction truly aligns to the UDL framework" (Smith & Basham, 2014).

COMMUNITY COLLEGES

The teaching method is already working at community colleges in the sense that many of their students would not be able to attend classes otherwise. According to Jaggars (2011), some of the advantages of online courses include an increase in the number of courses offered, time saved by not having to drive to school, and more flexibility in student schedules (as cited in Travers, 2016). Ivy Technical Community College in Indiana had more online students than any other community college in 2017 ("Ivy Tech Community College," 2017).

Ivy Tech's vice president of Academic Innovation and Support Kara Monroe touted the flexibility the college's online offerings gave students: "At Ivy Tech students can enjoy the convenience of online classes with the added support of on ground educational resources giving them the best of both worlds" ("Ivy Tech Community College," 2017).

Holder said at Surry Community College master online courses are created for every subject and updated every three years (C. Holder, personal communication, July 12, 2019). "Instructors cannot change the content which allows them to spend their time teaching and engaging students" (C. Holder, personal communication, July 12, 2019). Perhaps colleges and universities with low success rates might consider such a model.

UNIVERSITIES

Stewart, Goodson, Miertschin, Norwood, and Ezell (2013) indicated that support services were important for the success of online students. A definition of student services is "the academic, administrative, social, and psychological policies and practices to enable and facilitate student success" (Stewart et al., 2013, p. 292). The University of Houston's Retailing and Customer Service program decided it would revamp its online offerings, focusing more on services students needed to be successful. Stewart et al. (2013) found that student support in the areas of admissions, advising, academic supports, scholarships, library resources, articulation agreements, and career placements were needed for online university students.

The University of Houston provided support services needed by online students through its Instructional Support Services Center (Stewart et al., 2013). At the request of the Retailing and Customer Service program, the Instructional Support Services Center added online tutoring. Additionally, the university's Academic Services Center provided online academic counseling for students. Technical services personnel supported technology needs of faculty (Stewart et al., 2013).

Employed Students

Wolff, Wood-Kustanowitz, and Ashkenazi (2014) found that working students, in particular, needed outside supports more than students who did not work. The authors also determined that working students needed more guidance at registration, so that they entered their online course with realistic expectations. Additionally, "online student success rates could be enhanced by discouraging students with poor academic skills from enrolling in online courses" (Wolff et al., 2014, p. 174).

Western Governor's University (WGU) was started in 1997 when a group of politicians wanted to give more access to those who desired to attend college (WGU, 2019). The group of governors wished to remove the "boundaries to time and space" that hindered some from attending college (WGU, 2019). According to the 2018 WGU Annual Report, over 110,000 students attended WGU in 2018. Rather than using a time-bound system (such as a 16-week semester), WGU uses competency-based education, in which students can move at their own pace (WGU, 2019).

In other words, a student completes the course when he/she shows competency in the different skills required for completion of the class. If this takes only three weeks, the student can then move on to the next course. According to the 2018 WGU Annual Report, 50% of WGU students graduated in six years, compared to the national average of 38%. This high success rates suggest that competency-based education might be a better model for online students than a traditional, time-bound semester.

ONLINE EDUCATION'S FUTURE IN HIGHER EDUCATION

While many students have gotten over initial hesitation about taking online courses, many educators are concerned about the lack of student success. It can be said that the first phase of distance education was concerned with growth; the second phase will focus on evaluation, refinement, and improvement. It is assumed that if faculty members know how to teach in a traditional environment, they will also be able to teach in an online environment.

Faculty Issues

However, according to Young and Duncan (2014), "one of the largest challenges that instructors face is how to teach effectively in this relatively new online environment" (p. 70). While the basics might be covered in a training, it was found that faculty are often forced to teach themselves how to function effectively in an online environment (Shelton and Salsman (2005) as cited in Batts, Pagliari, Mallett, & McFadden, 2010). Researchers found that traditional methods that have worked in the seated classroom do not always work in an online environment (Gonzalez (2009), Horspool and Lange (2012) and Mayne and Wu (2011) as cited in Young & Duncan, 2014).

Student Issues

Not only are students less successful in online courses, but they tend to be less satisfied with them as well. Duncan (2005) and Young (2006) determined that students who had positive experiences in online courses felt their instructors "were concerned about their students, established trusting relationships, and provided structure and flexibility" (Young & Duncan, 2014). However, it was found that students not satisfied with online courses felt overwhelmed, bored, and disconnected because their instructors did not do a good job of communicating or engaging students (Borup, West, and Graham (2012) and Reilly et al. (2012) as cited in Young & Duncan, 2014).

Wolff et al. (2014) determined that there were factors such as course load, employment, job status, and caregiver status could make community college students less likely to succeed in an online environment. The authors also looked at the make-up of community college students, determining that "online students were significantly older and more likely to be employed than face-to-face (F2F) students. Online students were also more likely to describe themselves as the primary caregiver to a dependent child or adult" (Wolff et al., 2014, p. 171).

Needs for Faculty Training

One area of improvement could be in faculty training, which includes best practices (Batts et al., 2010). "Online programs and courses thrive when an institution makes available the necessary financial, human, and infrastructure resources required to design, maintain, and support online training programs" (Wolf (1999) as cited in Batts et al., 2010). Batts et al. (2010) recommended distance education administrators develop web-based training modules for their faculty. Other suggestions for training included assessment, consistent monitoring of assignments and discussion forums, and providing prompt feedback for students (Batts et al., 2010).

Another area of improvement could be in instruction. According to Jaggars and Xu (2016), "the effectiveness of online learning may vary according to how the online course is designed and taught, particularly among less-privileged student populations" (p. 270). In a study, Jaggars and Xu (2016) found that interaction between student and teacher seemed to have the biggest impact on student success. "Increased interpersonal interaction within the framework of the course, either with the instructor or with student peers, positively affects student learning" (Jaggars & Xu, 2015, p. 273).

Jaggars and Xu (2016) found that how much a student engaged with online discussion forums closely correlated with student success. The theory of transactional distance indicated that less interaction between the instructor and the student would make it more difficult for that student to succeed (Jaggars & Xu, 2016). One online student said: "Some teachers, they just don't care. Like you're on your own, like you're online, like it doesn't matter" (Jaggars & Xu, 2016, p. 278).

The Interactive Teacher

The highly interactive teacher does make her students feel like she cares through interaction. In addition, students who feel like their instructors are invested in them are more likely to succeed. According to Jaggars & Xu, some techniques of highly interactive instructors included frequent posts in discussion forums and on announcement pages, quick response to e-mails, asking for student feedback, and communicating with students using different modes (Jaggars & Xu, 2016).

"The strategies above seemed to help students to feel that the instructor cared about the course and students' performance in the course, which in turn helped students personalize the instructor, feel connected to the course, and strengthen their motivation to learn and succeed" (Jaggars & Xu, 2016, p. 278).

FUTURE SUCCESS

For distance education to remain a viable form of instruction, student success rates should be increased. To achieve higher student success, faculty should be trained on being highly interactive with their students, which has been proven to increase engagement (Jaggars & Xu, 2016). Accomplished and experienced online instructors can help administrators and distance education staff to train their fellow faculty members on how to engage students in online courses. Faculty are more likely to listen to their peers rather than a career administrator who has not been in the classroom for some time.

Joosten, Cusatsis, and Harness (2018) suggested that the creation of the National Research Center for Distance Education and Technological Advancements (DETA) could hasten innovative practices that could lead to increased student success. Despite the difference in format, it was found that there were no significant differences between the way teachers approached face-to-face and online classes. The main goal of DETA, established in 2014, is to locate the factors that determine whether a student is successful in an online class (Joosten et al., 2018).

Research Tool Kit

A research tool kit was devised to "guide individuals and institutions across the country in conducting research and collecting data on distance education and technological advancement" (Joosten et al., 2018, p. 11). Next, DETA solicited research from said institutions (Joosten et al., 2018). This data "led to the production of effective-use cases for instructional improvement, including the identification of success factors in distance and competency-based education" (Joosten et al., 2018, p.12).

The research conducted by DETA could do a great deal in helping instructors to design and teach courses that engage students, thus increasing success rates. However, for that to happen, faculty and administrators have to know about the database. Additionally, administrators have to put a priority on academic research, something that has traditionally been more important at universities than community colleges, which do not typically have a tenure system that requires publication of scholarly articles.

DISTANCE EDUCATION'S FUTURE USES IN K–12 ONLINE CHARTER SCHOOLS

The CRPE report asserts that online charter schools will only be a viable option in the future if they are further regulated (Pazhouh et al., 2015). According to the CRPE report, "few states have created intentional and robust regulatory environments for online charter schools" (Pazhouh et al., 2015, p.15). The CRPE report indicated that online charter schools should be more transparent in their data, develop more imaginative funding structures, and change policies of enrollment (Pazhouh et al., 2015).

The report points out that few states require online charter schools to provide data on "student attendance, progress, performance, and enrollment" (Pazhouh et al., 2015, p. 15). The CRPE report suggested online charter schools be made to create assessment plans detailing how student success would be measured. The report also suggested that states who have a completion-based funding model share their results with states who do not, so those states could evaluate whether that method would be best (Pazhouh et al., 2015).

The CRPE report recommended that states end open enrollment policies and "require schools to establish criteria for admission in order to ensure quality and effectiveness" (Pazhouh et al., 2015, p. 16). While the viability of online charter schools is currently in question, if regulation is increased, this might be a sound educational model in the future.

WHY STUDENTS ARE DRAWN TO THE TEACHING METHOD

K–12 Schools

Anyone who has seen a teenager who seems to have been glued to their phone and/or iPad could easily see why K–12 students would be drawn to a teaching method that utilizes technology. Pazhouh et al. (2015) found that K–12 students in rural areas and those with health problems stood to benefit from online courses. Gagnon and Mattingly (2016) deduced that since students who take AP classes are more likely to succeed in college, greater access through online AP programs helps disadvantaged students.

However, studies indicating lack of student success in K–12 online courses are troubling. While it is obvious to see why K–12 students would be drawn to the method, more time should be spent analyzing why so many students at this level are unsuccessful in online classes. Additionally, more research is needed into methods for engaging K–12 students in online courses. Finally, more of an effort should be made to accommodate students who have English as a second language and students with disabilities.

Community Colleges and Universities

It makes perfect sense that community college and university students would be drawn to online education. It was estimated that 57% of college students had at least a part-time job (Miller, Danner, and Staten (2008) as cited in Wolff et al., 2014). Students who work generally have less time than those who do not, so online courses offer a flexibility in scheduling that is attractive. Travers (2016) posited that it was no surprise that community colleges taught a large number of online classes when one considered how many of their students were working adults who had numerous responsibilities outside of the classroom.

Time Constraints

Unfortunately, these time constraints could lower their chances of success. "These students are impacted by factors outside the school context that takes time away from course work" (Travers, 2016, p. 50). Community college administrators have seen distance education as an opportunity to enroll traditionally underrepresented students (Travers, 2016).

Demographic Issues

However, Xu, and Jaggars (2011, 2014) found that the underrepresented students, such as African Americans and Hispanics were far less successful in online courses than they were in traditional courses (as cited in Travers, 2016). According to a 2000 survey by the National Educational Association, interaction between faculty and students goes up in online courses (as cited in Batts et al., 2010). However, this is only true in some courses. In courses in which students feel disengaged from the instructor, students are more likely to be unsuccessful in the course (Jaggars & Xu, 2016).

WGU gets high marks in student engagement. According to the 2018 National Survey of Student Engagement, 74% of WGU students said they had very good/excellent interactions with faculty members as compared to the national average of 55% (as cited in WGU 2018 Annual Report).

The 2018 WGU Annual Report boasts that 71% of their students fall into the category of "underserved." Considering this school's high graduation rate and 97% student satisfaction rate (WGU 2018 Annual Report), perhaps one answer to increasing success rates for minority online students is to offer competency-based education. Seventy-two percent of WGU students strongly agreed or agreed with the statement that the school was "perfect . . . for people like me" (WGU 2018 Annual Report).

HOW DISTANCE EDUCATION ALIGNS WITH 21ST-CENTURY TECHNOLOGIES

Is it possible that one day a computer could teach online English composition? One need only take a cursory look at *Grammarly*, an application used by many community colleges and universities to find an answer. Not only does the AI-driven program make suggestions about grammar and punctuation, it also alerts users to issues involving plagiarism, style, tone, and wordiness (Grammarly, 2019). While the product does not quite make corrections for the user, the program makes it easy for users to implement its suggestions.

Dr. Candace Holder is part of an artificial intelligence experiment in the North Carolina Community College System (North Carolina Community College System, 2019). Surry Community College in collaboration with NCCCS and the North Carolina Virtual Learning Community determined "that machine learning is highly effective at mapping and organizing data resources without the necessity of moving data into one large data lake" (North Carolina Community College System, 2019). Surry has entered into a partnership with other North Carolina Community colleges to research the possibility of creating virtual research assistants to be used in online classes (North Carolina Community College System, 2019).

Online Tutoring

In 2016, IBM signed an agreement with textbook giant Pearson to offer online artificial intelligence tutoring. Not only does the program ask and answer questions as a face-to-face tutor would, it "provides instructors with insights about how well students are learning, allowing them to better manage the entire course and flag students who need help" (IBM, 2016).

According to Crowe, LaPierre, and Kebritchi (2017), systems like Watson "encompass the major components of one-to-one interaction between the instructor and learners, customized instructions based on learners' needs, and individual feedback for the learners" (p. 497). One aim of the program is to provide support for students who have busy work, school, and home schedules (IBM, 2016).

Various researchers have shown that success rates in online classes lag behind those in traditional classes. Perhaps artificial intelligence, if not fully teaching online courses, could provide an aid for teachers in increasing student success. Sherry Gross, a professor of economics at University of South

Carolina, Sumter, pointed out that the IBM Watson tutoring program is available 24 hours a day, seven days a week, even if she isn't (IBM, 2016). "I like the accessibility, mastery, reading and learning part of it," Grosso said (as cited in IBM Watson Education, 2016).

A 2013 study by Steenbergen-Hu and Cooper indicated that intelligent tutoring systems, or tutoring done by artificial intelligence, had a significant impact on student learning. This impact was not as great as human tutoring (Steenbergen-Hu & Cooper, 2013), but many online students do not have the option of having human tutoring. It was found that artificial intelligence tutoring increased student performance beyond human tutoring (Kulik and Fletcher (2016) as cited in Crowe et al., 2017). Van Lehn (2011) found only marginal differences between face-to-face human tutoring and artificial intelligence tutoring.

Van Lehn (2011) indicated that the use of artificial intelligence tutoring should be increased and refined, indicating "we may soon see self-improving tutoring systems that monitor their own processes and outcomes in order to modify their tutoring tactics and make them more effective" (p. 213). Humans take much longer to improve because they are not given the constant stream of data and feedback that a computer tutor is given (VanLehn, 2011). Steenbergen-Hu and Cooper (2013) found that how the teachers administered the tutoring, and the pedagogical underpinning of the tutoring had an important impact on student success, showing the importance of the human teacher using the tool correctly.

Crowe et al. (2017) emphasized that augmented intelligence, rather than artificial intelligence, will be the next major factor in education. The researchers pointed out that while artificial intelligence aims to replicate human behavior, augmented intelligence serves as a problem-solving aid for humans. Resistance from educators in part results from a confusion over the role of the two intelligences (Crowe et al., 2017).

Instructional designers who show instructors the benefits of augmented intelligence, which include "virtually instantaneous feedback ... and ... real-time tutoring and assistance" (Crowe et al., 2017, p. 495) can mitigate this confusion. Crowe et al. (2017) agreed with Steenbergen-Hu (2013) that artificial intelligence tools could help online students deal with time-management issues, a major determinant of lack of success.

CONCLUSION

In conclusion, online education is already working for many K–12, community college and university students in the sense that the format opens doors for students who may not otherwise be able to take classes. However, the focus of online education needs to shift from access to success. Many studies have indicated that students are less successful in online classes than they are in traditional classes. Low success rates for students enrolled in corporately run online K–12 programs are particularly troubling because they suggest that the companies are more interested in profit than they are in student success.

The door is open for a new wave of innovation in which students are engaged by online courses. WGU's high success rates indicate that competency-based education is a format worth pursuing for other schools. Online programs at the K–12, community college, and university levels will need to deal with the implications of artificial intelligence. School administrators should educate themselves about the pros and cons of artificial intelligence, determining how it can be used most effectively.

CHAPTER SUMMARY

- Online education continues to grow rapidly.
- Critics are concerned with assessment of charter school quality.
- Community colleges have led the way in developing online courses serving students who are working and sometimes full-time caretakers.
- Online classes afford students the opportunity to enroll in classes they might not otherwise take.
- Online programs typically use LMSs.
- Quality Matters provides professional development for faculty who teach online.
- The Online Learning Consortium holds a national conference providing resources.
- In K–12 education, online course provide opportunities for students who might not normally have access.
- In 2016 researchers found that 51.4% of rural school districts offered AP classes, while 93.8% of suburban and 97.3% of urban district did.
- Online courses have become attractive to students with disabilities.
- Community colleges find that students who might not otherwise be able to attend traditional classes were enrolling in online classes.
- At the university level it was found that support services were important for success of online students.
- Students who were working needed more support than those who did not work.
- WGU was started in 1997 when a group of politicians wanted to give more access to those who desired to attend college.

- WGU uses competency-based education, in which student can move at their own pace.
- Many educators are concerned about the lack of student success.
- Not only are student less successful in online courses, but they tend to be less satisfied with them as well.
- Student reported the faculty did not do a good job of communicating or engaging students.
- Faculty training could help using best practices.
- Researchers found that interaction between student and teacher seemed to have the biggest impact on student success.
- For online education to remain a viable form of instruction, student success rates should be increased.
- Researchers found that there were not significant differences between the way teachers approached face-to-face and online classes.
- More research is needed at the community college level on distance education courses.
- Teenagers are drawn to a teaching method that uses technology.
- Community college students who are working are more likely to access online courses.
- Research has shown that African Americans and Hispanics were far less successful in online courses than they were in traditional courses.
- One possible answer to increasing success rates for minority online students is to offer competency-based education.
- In the future artificial intelligence may teach almost any course, including English Composition.
- Artificial Intelligence may provide an aid to the traditional teacher in the near future.
- Online education is already working for many K–12, community college, and university students in the sense that the format opens doors for students who may not otherwise be able to take classes.
- Competency-based instruction may be the format that needs to be used in online courses.

NOTE

1. Editor's Note: Online Education has been an educational option for decades. It has made significant inroads into education by providing a variety of teaching options. Time and inventiveness will undoubtedly bring this teaching method to its full potential.

REFERENCES

Batts, D., Pagliari, L., Mallett, W., & McFadden, C. (2010). Training for faculty who teach online. *The Community College Enterprise, 16*(2), 21–31. Retrieved from http://nclive.org/cgi-bin/nclsm?url=http://search.proquest.com/docview/8131 35201?accountid=13190.

Crowe, D., Lapierre, M., & Kebritchi, M. (2017). Knowledge based artificial augmentation intelligence technology: Next step in academic instructional tools for distance learning. *TechTrends, 61*(5), 494–506. doi: http://dx.doi.org/10.1007/s115 28-017-0210-4.

Fenty, N. S., & Allio, A. (2017). Using distance learning to impact access of diverse learners to advanced placement programs. *Quarterly Review of Distance Education, 18*(2), 39–56. Retrieved from http://nclive.org/cgi-bin/nclsm?url=http://se arch.proquest.com/docview/1955987034?accountid=13190.

Gagnon, D. J., & Mattingly, M. J. (2016). Advanced placement and rural schools: Access, success, and exploring alternatives the journal of secondary gifted education JSGE. *Journal of Advanced Academics, 27*(4), 266–284. doi: http://dx.doi.o rg/10.1177/1932202X16656390.

Grammarly. (2019). *FAQ*. Retrieved from https://www.grammarly.com/faq#toc0.

IBM. (2016, October 25). *IBM Watson and Pearson to drive cognitive learning experiences for college students*. Retrieved from https://www 03.ibm.com/press/us/ en/pressrelease/50842.wss+&cd=1&hl=en&ct=clnk&gl=us&client=firefox-b-1-d.

Ivy Tech Community College ranked top community college with students enrolled in distance education. (2017, June 5). *Targeted News Service*. Retrieved from http: //nclive.org/cgi-bin/nclsm?url=http://search.proquest.com/docview/190608636 8?accountid=13190.

Jaggars, S. S., & Xu, D. (2016). How do online course design features influence student performance? *Computers & Education, 95*(1), 270–284.

Joosten, T., Cusatis, R., & Harness, L. (2018). Research innovation in distance education. *Planning for Higher Education, 46*(3), 8–17. Retrieved from http://nclive. org/cgi-bin/nclsm?url=http://search.proquest.com/docview/2078623812?accounti d=13190.

North Carolina Community College System. (2019, June 27). *The NC brain workshop*. Online Learning Consortium, 2016.

Pazhouh, R., Lake, R., & Miller, L. (2016, 4). A policy framework for online charter schools. *The Education Digest, 81*, 49–57. Retrieved from http://nclive.org/cgi-bin /nclsm?url=http://search.proquest.com/docview/1768622862?accountid=13190.

Qualitymatters.org/ga-resources/rubric-standards (2016).

Smith, S. J., & Basham, J. D. (2014). Designing online learning opportunities for students with disabilities. *Teaching Exceptional Children, 46*(5), 127–137. Retrieved from http://nclive.org/cgi-bin/nclsm?url=http://search.proquest.com/docview/1552 688737?accountid=13190.

Steenbergen-Hu, S., & Cooper, H. (2014). A meta-analysis of the effectiveness of intelligent tutoring systems on college students' academic learning. *Journal of*

Educational Psychology, 106(2), 331. Retrieved from http://nclive.org/cgi-bin/nclsm?url=http://search.proquest.com/docview/1523712755?accountid=13190.

Stewart, B. L., Goodson, C. E., Miertschin, S. L., Norwood, M. L., & Ezell, S. (2013). Online student support services: A case based on quality frameworks. *Journal of Online Learning and Teaching, 9*(2), 290. Retrieved from http://nclive.org/cgi-bin/nclsm?url=http://search.proquest.com/docview/1500422198?accountid=13190.

Strauss, V. (2015, October 31). Study on online charter schools: "It is literally as if the kid did not go to school for an entire year." *Washington Post.* Retrieved from https://www.washingtonpost.com/news/answer-sheet/wp/2015/10/31/study-on-online-charter-schools-it-is-literally-as-if-the-kid-did-not-go-to-school-for-an-entire-year/?noredirect=on&utm_term=.bb42a898a931.

Travers, S. (2016). Supporting online student retention in community colleges: What data is most relevant? *Quarterly Review of Distance Education, 17*(4), 49–61, 76. Retrieved from http://nclive.org/cgi-bin/nclsm?url=http://search.proquest.com/docview/1891317891?accountid=13190.

VanLehn, K. (2011). The relative effectiveness of human tutoring, intelligent tutoring systems, and other tutoring systems. *Educational Psychologist, 46*(4), 197. Retrieved from http://nclive.org/cgi-bin/nclsm?url=http://search.proquest.com/docview/900807152?accountid=13190.

Young, S., & Duncan, H. E. (2014). Online and face-to-face teaching: How do student ratings differ? *Journal of Online Learning and Teaching, 10*(1), 70-n/a. Retrieved from http://nclive.org/cgi-bin/nclsm?url=http://search.proquest.com/docview/1614680708?accountid=13190.

Western Governor's University. (2019). *Education without boundaries.* Retrieved from https://www.wgu.edu/about/our-story.html.

Western Governor's University. (2018). *WGU 2018 annual report* (2018). Retrieved from https://www.wgu.edu/content/dam/western-governors/documents/annual-report/annual-report-2018.pdf.

Wolff, B. G., Wood-Kustanowitz, A., & Ashkenazi, J. M. (2014). Student performance at a community college: Mode of delivery, employment, and academic skills as predictors of success. *Journal of Online Learning and Teaching, 10*(2), 166-n/a. Retrieved from http://nclive.org/cgi-bin/nclsm?url=http://search.proquest.com/docview/1614680177?accountid=13190.

Chapter 4

The Flipped Classroom Education[1]

Darrel W. Staat

AN EXPERIENCE

Some six decades ago, an eighth-grade English teacher who had never heard of the flipped classroom became aware after a few months of teaching that teachers do not teach, students learn. After that epiphany, he directed a play version of Charles Dickens's *A Christmas Carol* with eighth graders as actors, set designers and builders, costume designers and developers. All went well. The parents and friends came to see the production just before Christmas and enjoyed it. In addition, the students got very excited about their success.

As a result they came to the teacher and asked if they could write a play and produce it. That creative project fit into the literature course he was teaching, although it was a very unusual way to conduct the course. However, since the students were so motivated and excited about writing and producing their own play, the teacher agreed.

The students worked after school, at home, and in groups in class with their ideas, plot scripts, set design and costumes. The teacher guided them on a variety of levels including the structure of the plot, the development of the characters, the tone of the script, the meaning of the play, and the like. When the script was completed, he held auditions to determine which students would play the parts.

Since not all members of the class were needed as actors, a number of the students helped to design and build the set, often with assistance from their fathers who got interested in the project. Other students helped design costumes with help from encouraging mothers. Those acting in the play learned their parts and practiced them. The teacher worked as a manager throughout the process.

As the semester progressed, the rehearsals went well, the set was constructed, and the costumes completed. The play was presented in the late spring semester to parents and friends. The entire project came off as a big success. Students learned a great deal about drama, parents loved seeing what their children had created, and the teacher was proud to be a guide throughout the process. The teacher now understands that he used a flipped classroom experience that worked successfully.

FROM ONE CENTURY TO THE NEXT

The 21st century is probably assumed by most people in the civilized world to be a continuation of the previous century. But is that an accurate assumption? The computer by itself created serious change for the 21st century, even though types of mechanical computers have been around for a very long time. Back in 1822, Charles Babbage invented a mechanical calculator he called the Difference Machine (Ranjan, 2016). Although it was completely designed and a model constructed, the Babbage machine was not produced during his lifetime.

More recently, during World War II, computers were installed to assist naval fighting vessels to track incoming aircraft and successfully shoot them down. Those computers were large and bulky; their abilities were narrowly focused, but they got the job done. After the war, in 1946, the Electrical Numerical Integrator And Calculator (ENIAC) was designed and built. It was located in a huge, cooled room, used multiple vacuum tubes, and was developed to solve simple mathematical problems, which it could do in short order (Levy, 2013). Change was in the air in the 1950s, but it took decades for its affect to be felt across the board; how did that come about?

Moore's Law

It took the ability to place a single transistor on a chip the size of a person's thumbnail in 1957 to begin a computer revolution that blossomed rapidly. By the mid-1960s, Gordon Moore, one of the founders of Intel, stated that he thought the number of transistors per chip was doubling every two years. Thus, Moore's Law was initiated (Templeton, 2015). That doubling process has continued to the present. In 2019, Intel predicts it will place the equivalent of 100 billion transistors on a chip of thumb nail size. The doubling process over the decades also meant computer power and computer storage doubled at the same rate.

Moore's Law explains why the bag-phone of the early 1990s became the iPhone of 2007 and later, the iPhone 11 of 2019. The latter is actually a powerful handheld computer with an integrated phone. Moore's Law explains where Facebook, Twitter, and Instagram came from and why Uber and Airbnb were possible. In addition, that doubling process over decades allows for the Internet of Things (IoT), 3D printing, autonomous vehicles, personal robots, artificial intelligence, nanotechnology, genome development, crypto currency and the like to become realities in just a matter of a few years. Anyone born after 1990, Generation Z, grew up with these diverse technologies already existing. They seem normal to Zers.

Twenty-First-Century Students

Twenty-first-century students are different from their 20th-century counterparts. They are what has been called "digital natives" Marc Prensky (as cited in Magana, 2017). Today's students have grown up with computers, iPads, smartphones, the Internet, and social media. They accept them, and more to come, as normal. The technologies have always existed as far as digital natives are concerned. Since they have been using digital technology all of their lives so far, they expect that when they go to a community college or a university that those media, and more, will be integral parts of the educational process.

Most teachers and professors, on the other hand, have been educated using print material found in libraries and bookstores. The various technologies are viewed as something new, but are without full acceptance. Educators in the early 21st century are described as "digital immigrants." Many of them understand digital technology more as a nuisance than a valuable asset to be used in the education process (Marc Prensky as cited in Magana, 2017). Consequently, a technology, such as the smartphone, is seen as an object needed to be kept under control and not to be used in the classroom.

Although it seems obvious to the digital native that 21st-century technologies should be an integral part of their educational process, the digital immigrants are not on board and tend to think that these new technologies should be effectively controlled. However, it is gradually becoming recognized that educating students using past methods will not meet the requirements for graduates' success in the future. The classroom has to change.

THE FLIPPED CLASSROOM METHOD

The flipped classroom is a possibility to meet the demands of the change. Using that pedagogy, the instructor is no longer the "sage-on-the-stage" but becomes the "guide on the side" (Alison King as cited in Rhoeling, 2018, p. 3). The instructor's role becomes that of a designer, learning manager, tutor, clarifier, and problem solver. In the 21st century, the pedagogy of lecture/discussion is a more limited learning process. There may be times when that method, dating back to the Greeks, works for specific situations, but in general, it most likely will fade into the background as the teacher, instructor, and professor take on the role of an educated guide helping to lead students in the proper direction.

Although the concept of the flipped classroom may have been used in the past by individual instructors, it has taken until the 21st century for the method to become a reality used by a number of educators from K–12 to graduate programs. There are numerous articles and books written on the topic as this method of teaching is rapidly becoming recognized. The early notions of the flipped classroom can be found in the work of John Dewey in the early 20th century, but its acceptance into mainstream teaching has taken until the 21st century (Wheeler, 2016).

Definition

What is the flipped classroom? "As currently described, a flipped classroom is one in which foundational information of the course is moved outside of the classroom through readings, recorded mini lectures, and videos. Class time is then used to help students apply the information through in-class activities, working through problems, or engaging in higher levels of critical thinking" (Blythe, Sweet, & Carpenter, 2015, p. 2). The flipped classroom puts the focus for learning on the students, who before entering the classroom, have already investigated the assigned information on their own through readings, videos, blogs, Internet, and/or other sources of learning.

Short Videos

Many instructors who use the flipped classroom find that short videos, made by the instructor or accessed from an external source work very well for today's students who come to school with broad experience in 21st-century technologies through the use of PCs, smartphones, social media, and video games (Bergman & Sams, 2012). Since so much information on almost any topic exists digitally and students already use some segments of it in their daily lives, the flipped classroom can be a successful way to use their knowledge and experience with technology when they enter the classroom.

EXPERIENCE OF A PROFESSOR

A member of the faculty at the Wingate University in the Physical Therapy Department has successfully used the flipped classroom method. Before coming to Wingate in January 2019, she was a member of the faculty at the New York Institute of Technologies (NYIT) located on Long Island for twenty years. Her eight years' experience with the flipped classroom was in an orthopedic course she taught.

Rationale

The course used lecture/demonstration to teach both theory and practice, which meant significant, hands-on clinical activity. She found the scheduled class time was never long enough time to include both lecture/demonstration and student practice of the critical physical therapy procedures they needed to learn. She decided to flip the classroom; she created videos demonstrating the proper procedures that the student would watch before coming to class (K. Friel, personal communication, May 7, 2019).

In class the students demonstrated their skills with the procedure while the instructor observed. Improper procedures were pointed out, further demonstration given as needed, and the student practiced repeatedly. Using the class time this way, she found she could work with students individually, and for longer periods of time to help them increase their clinical competence. When needed, she would stop the students and give a lecture on common problems or errors she was observing, and then allow the students to practice further (K. Friel, personal communication, May 7, 2019).

Results

She found two results from flipping the classroom. One, the students did better on assessments than students who had experienced the traditional lecture/demonstration method. And two, she found that the students did better on the certification testing. The instructor went further and developed an e-textbook for the student to use before they came to class. Her written instructions assisted student learning even more and allowed her to flip both the lecture and lab portions of the course. She became a very strong proponent of the flipped classroom and used it for eight years (K. Friel, personal communication, May 7, 2019).

When the New York Institute of Technology contracted with a school in Ammaen Jordan to teach a physical therapy program there, the instructor used her videos online. During the class sessions, an onsite coordinator worked with the students face-to-face assisting them to practice and appropriately learn the procedures much as the instructor had done at NYIT. The program successfully taught Jordanian students using the online program (K. Friel, personal communication, May 7, 2019).

Student Reaction

When asked how the students reacted to the flipped classroom, the professor acknowledged that initially some students liked the method, while others did not. In order to make sure the students had actually watched the videos in preparation for the class session, the professor initially started each class with a short quiz. She reported that as time went by most students learned to see the value of the videos even though they were hesitant at first. By the second semester, all students had adjusted to the teaching method and used it successfully (K. Friel, personal communication, May 7, 2019).

Faculty Reaction

She said that over time more professionally produced videos were on the market and some of them worked even better than professor-created videos. She also found that other faculty were not always as enamored with the method as she was. In order to flip the classroom, one has to give up the lecturing reins and move to the guide on the side rather than the sage-on-the-stage (K. Friel, personal communication, May 7, 2019).

TWENTY-FIRST-CENTURY TECHNOLOGY

Since the 21st century has a considerable amount of technology available to students and is being used by them, it seems logical that educators should take advantage of the possibilities they have created. These days most college students already carry a powerful computer with them daily in the form of a cell phone. Why not experiment at least with using that cornucopia of information? Videos used in the flipped classroom make sense. It allows the student to learn more accurately and rapidly than the traditional classroom methods.

DEVELOPING THE FLIPPED CLASSROOM

So, how does one go about developing a flipped classroom? For background there are a considerable number of books on the topic. Most are personal experiences faculty members in high schools and undergraduate institutions have had and there are a few that have been seriously researched on the higher education level as well.

In general, those using the flipped classroom successfully would give the following advice: first, find topics in the course being taught that could successfully use the flipped classroom approach. In other words, determine what would work best with a traditional teaching method and what would make sense to use the flipped method. For topics best thought to use the flipped method, decide how the class session would be changed to take advantage of that pre-class learning (Roehling, 2018).

Second, do not jump at once into everything being taught using the flipped classroom. Experiment with certain topics that might work better with the flipped method. As experience is gained and feedback considered from the students, move on to other topics. There is a considerable amount of work on the instructor's part preparing for such a significant change. However, once the change is made, the instructor will find it easier to move forward with more topics. The reaction of the students for or against the method will assist the instructor to decide whether the method is working or not (Blythe et al., 2015).

Third, those experienced with the flipped method often find that working with another faculty member(s) is very helpful in the development, implementation, and the assessment of the method. Having a partner can help a great deal when moving through difficult times in the process of development (Bergman et al., 2013). Finally, the pleasure of developing a method that works well with students is a very compelling motivation to continue on. The process is analogous to learning how to swim; at the beginning it is difficult, but as one learns the process, it becomes enjoyable and fun.

EXPERIENCE AT THE SECONDARY LEVEL

Today the flipped classroom method is being used at the high school and higher education levels. Jonathan Bergman and Aaron Sams, both high school science teachers, wrote a book describing how they initiated a flipped classroom and then developed it over the years into a highly successful method of teaching. They developed videos for the students to watch at home that covered the foundational materials for the class period. In class they worked with students in groups and individually to help them with any misunderstood concepts in a tutoring fashion (Bergman et al., 2012).

What the two faculty members liked about the process was that they got to talk to almost every student in each class period rather than lecturing to the class as a whole. By communicating directly with each student, they found who needed help understanding the basics and who they could direct to supporting information for further study (Bergman et al., 2012). An interesting thing happened when talking to parents at teacher-parent conferences: the teacher found the parents were watching the videos right along with their children, and the parents really liked the experience (Bergman et al., 2012).

Over the years Bergman and Sams developed a set of components for a successful flipped classroom which included the following:

- Establish clear learning objectives.
- Determine which of these objectives are best achieved through inquiry, and which are best learned through direct instruction.
- Assure student access to videos.
- Incorporate engaging learning activities to be done in class.
- Create multiple versions of each summative assessment for students to demonstrate their mastery of each learning objective in a particular unit of study (Bergman et al., 2012).

This basic set of components, along with a considerable amount of discussion of other information gleaned from a number of years of conducing flipped classrooms, is contained in Bergman and Sams's book (2012). The experience and growth of these two authors are considerable. They bring a wealth of information to the teacher, instructor, and professor who are interested in learning more about this teaching method.

Explaining the Flipped Classroom to Students

Once the decision has been made by the instructor to move to the flipped classroom, Bergman and Sams (2012) suggest that the course should begin by introducing the student to flipped model. Be prepared to answer questions and explain why the flipped method is most beneficial to the student. Let them know right from the beginning what the teaching method will be and why it is important. They also caution that the first time may be the most difficult, but by the second year, the bugs can be worked out and things move along smoothly (Bergman et al., 2012).

The Use of Videos

Bergman and Sams (2012) also suggest that the instructor should take time to teach the student how to watch videos for the course and how to take effective notes on the topic being discussed. They also suggest encouraging the students to help each other as the focus of the course is not on the instructor, but rather on student learning. Groups working together externally and in-class motivate them to complete assignments as well as to learn increasing independently.

Importance of the Syllabus

Blythe, Sweet, and Carpenter (2015) remind the instructor to flip the syllabus for the course. Present the flipped syllabus to the students on day one of the course, or before, so they have an idea of what is coming. Hold an online quiz on the contents of the syllabus to make sure everyone understands the process and expectations of the course. "The syllabus is the first impression student have of your course" (Blythe et al., p. 5).

Identifying Goals

Roehling (2018) suggests that the instructor should encourage the students to "Identify the goals for the course" (p. 108). She recommends the class be divided into small groups and the students discuss why they are taking the course and what specifically they want to learn from the course. She also sees the need for the instructor to explain the student responsibilities in class and pre-class assignment. Further, she discusses the importance of carefully defining the role of the instructor in the flipped classroom (Roehling, 2018).

ROOKIE MISTAKES

Honeycutt (2016) lists seven "rookie mistakes" when preparing for the flipped classroom: "*Rookie Mistake #1:* Narrowly defining what the flipped classroom is" (Honeycutt, 2016, p. 24). It is important the instructor carefully analyze what and why they are using the flipped method. "Involve students in higher level learning and critical thinking experiences *during* class time. Move lower level learning experiences *outside* of class time" (Honeycutt, 2016, p. 24).

"*Rookie Mistake #2:* Poorly articulated learning outcomes" (Honeycutt, 2016, p. 25). The instructor must take the time needed to clearly explain what the learning outcomes are for the course and how the activities in the course focus on the learning outcomes.

"*Rookie Mistake #3:* Not planning" (Honeycutt, 2016, p. 25). The instructor needs to carefully plan the learning outcomes and how the activities, assignments, and experiences help the students obtain those outcomes.

"*Rookie Mistake #4:* The activity is too big" (Honeycutt, 2016, p. 25). Too often an instructor will jump into a major project for the class that is too complicated and difficult for the students to complete. It is much better to use a number of smaller projects that lead up to the larger one so that the students learn in a logical, step-by-step manner.

"*Rookie Mistake #5:* Flipping Everything" (Honeycutt, 2016, p. 26). Carefully analyze what has been used in the course previously and continue to use what has worked well. Do not throw the baby out with the bathwater. Use the flipped method where it will be of most value and benefit to the student's learning abilities.

"*Rookie Mistake #6:* Forgetting to prepare students for their changing role" (Honeycutt, 2016, p. 26). Be sure to carefully explain what the flipped classroom is all about and how it can benefit the student. Take the time needed to make sure the students understand the reasons for using the flipped classroom. Take time to answer their questions before moving ahead.

"*Rookie Mistake #7:* Forgetting to prepare for your changing role" (Honeycutt, 2016, p. 26). It is critical for the instructor to move from the center of attention in the class to focusing on student learning. The instructor is in a learning management position, the "guide on the side," which for many may be a very significant change in their teaching careers (Honeycutt, 2016, p. 26).

CONCLUSION

The flipped classroom is a teaching method that focuses on student learning. It helps the students become independent learners, those who know how to learn on their own. The skill of continuous learning, which in the 21st century of rapidly developing technologies and difficulties in adapting to them and their impact on education, careers, and life in general, is absolutely critical. The flipped classroom puts the responsibility on the student to learn rather that the teacher to expound. This change in focus is critical to the future success of the students after graduation as they enter and continue in their careers. The flipped classroom methodology provides a pathway to success for all concerned; as such, it is well worth investigating and putting into use.

CHAPTER SUMMARY

- Teachers do not teach; students learn.
- Eighth-grade students wrote and produced their own play.
- Charles Babbage and his Difference Machine.
- World War II's naval vessels used early computers.
- After the war, ENIAC is created.
- The development of the number of transistors on a chip led to Moore's Law.

- Moore's Law explains the development of Facebook, Twitter, Instagram, the iPhone 10, Uber, and Airbnb.
- Digital Natives in the 21st century and their counterparts, Digital Immigrants.
- Twenty-first-century technologies should be an integral part of the educational process.
- The flipped classroom changes the faculty member from the sage-on-the-stage to the guide on the side.
- Support for the flipped classroom can be found in the work of John Dewey.
- The flipped classroom puts the focus for learning on the students.
- Short videos created by the instructor work well in the flipped classroom.
- A professor used the flipped classroom in the teaching of physical therapy.
- Students watched faculty-made videos to learn hands-on procedures and practiced them in the class session.
- The entire course was taught successfully online to a school in Ammaen, Jordan.
- Student reaction to the flipped classroom varied from some liking it immediately to others coming along more slowly.
- Students' competence increased significantly using the flipped method over the traditional lecture/demonstration method.
- The 21st century brings many technologies that can be used in the classroom.
- Experienced faculty provide the following advice: start with certain topics; do not jump immediately into using the flipped classroom for everything; work with a faculty partner if possible, and the results will further motivate the faculty member to continue.
- Two science teachers, Bergman and Sams, have had great success with the flipped classroom.
- The two faculty members found they could work individually with students at almost every class session.
- They provided a set of components to follow for teachers interested in trying the flipped classroom concept.
- It is important to explain to students how the flipped classroom works right from the first class meeting.
- Teaching the students how to watch the videos and to take notes properly is important.
- The students need to have the complete syllabus for the course before the class begins or no later than the first day of class.
- Some faculty recommend that the students on a college level should be given the opportunity to discuss what they expect to learn from the flipped course.
- A set of seven "rookie mistakes" is provided by an experienced teacher using the flipped classroom.
- The flipped classroom is a teaching method that focuses on student learning.

NOTE

1. Editor's Note: The Flipped Classroom is referenced in various chapters of this book. The idea behind all of them is to find a way to focus learning on the student rather than from the instructor. It encourages understanding how to learn on one's own.

REFERENCES

Bergman, J., & Sams, A. (2012). *Flip your classroom: Reach every student in every class every day.* Eugene, Oregon: International Society for Technology in Education.

Blythe, H., Sweet, C., & Carpenter, R. (2015). *It works for me. Flipping the classroom: Shared tips for effective teaching.* Stillwater, Oklahoma: New Forums Press Inc.

Honeycutt, B. (Ed.). (2016). *Flipping the college classroom: Practical advice from faculty.* Madison, Wisconsin: Magna Publications.

Levy, S. (2013, November). The brief history of the ENIAC computer: A look back at the room-size governmental computer that began the digital era. *Smithsonian Magazine.* Retrieved from https://www.smithsonianmag.com/history/the-brief-history-of-the-eniac-computer-3889120/.

Magana, S. (2017). *Disruptive classroom technologies: A framework for innovation in education.* Thousand Oaks, California: Corwin.

Ranjan, A. (2016, February). Charles Babbage-Father of the computer. *Techtricksworld.* Retrieved from https://www.techtricksworld.com/charles-babbage/.

Roehling, P. (2018). *Flipping the college classroom: An evidence based guide.* Cham, Switzerland: Palgrave Pivot.

Templeton, G. (2015, July). What is Moore's Law? *Extreme Tech.* Retrieved from https://www.extremetech.com/extreme/210872-explains-what-is-moore's-law/.

Wheeler, S. (2016, January). *The pedagogy of John Dewey: A summary.* Teach Thought. Retrieved from https://www.teachthought.com/learning/pedagogy-john-dewey-summary/.

Chapter 5

Gaming Education[1]

Melisa Johnson

As discussed in the introduction of the text, a new method of learning and teaching is on the horizon. The new instructional method has to be more student-focused in order to engage those that have grown up with technology. Community colleges and universities will need to turn their focus from traditional classroom lectures to more digitally enhanced lectures such as gaming in order to meet the needs of the students and the business community in the 21st century.

Games have been long accepted as a way for children to learn how to interact with others, how to learn about the world in which they live, and how to behave. Educational games have been used by the military to teach strategy while simulation games have been common in corporate training for years. Academic research has been done on traditional, non-digital games for 40 years or longer; however, the use of digital games in academics is a relatively new concept (Whitton, 2014).

GAMES

Computers became commonplace for homes and businesses in the early 1980s. It was during this time that digital games in learning were introduced. The tools that are needed are much better and cheaper, and there is more clarity around problems that we are trying to solve (Ark & Wise, 2011).

Computer games have grown in many ways including in the field of educational learning. Games can make learning more fun for the students as well as provide an opportunity for creative thinking. Games will often trigger lively discussions among the students relating to the learning concepts following game play. Educational games are defined as games that are designed for teaching and learning. In these games, a student's motivation and engagement can be increased by combining the elements of fun and educational components. The learning process of students can be enhanced by two new ways of teaching: game-based learning and gamification (Al-Azawi, Al-Faliti, & Al-Blushi, 2016).

Although the terms "game-based learning" and "gamification" are often used interchangeably, each term is treated separately with specific emphasis on the use within education. Game-based learning is when "actual games are used in the classroom to enhance learning and teaching," and gamification is when "game-design elements are used in non-game contexts" (Wiggins, 2016, p. 18).

Game-Based Learning

Game-based learning is the intentional use of digital games to fulfill a specific learning objective in a more interesting way. Not only does it make the learning process more fun, it has a "positive effect on cognitive development" (Al-Azawi et al., 2016, p. 134). The traditional learning process may be considered boring; therefore, adding games to the traditional courses can improve the learning motivation of students. When students are given the opportunity to enter in a state of playing, their level of concentration tends to rise higher than normal. It makes the learning process more interesting and fun (Al-Azawi et al., 2016). As noted by Wiggins, adding digital games is an option to enhance curricula with the intent of maintaining attention and increasing knowledge retention (Wiggins, 2016).

Gamification

Gamification is defined as "the practice of using game design elements, game mechanics, and game thinking in non-game activities" (Al-Azawi et al., 2016, p. 133). Game-design elements are added to instruction in hopes of "incentivizing a particular process thereby adding intrinsic motivation in a given gamified process which invariably uses extrinsic rewards" (Wiggins, 2016, p. 20). Some of the game elements used are badges, trophies, rewards, and leader boards, which tap into people's natural desires for "competition, achievement, recognition and self-expression" (Al-Azawi et al., 2016, p. 133).

According to Wiggins (2016), gamification aspects are not completely new to curricula in terms of current strategies used to encourage extrinsic motivation. Gamification strategies in the classroom may not be as "novel as previously assumed" (p. 27). It appears that traditional instructional techniques are already being reworked using gamification or game-based learning strategies. Through the innovative use of digital games and simulations in classrooms, gamification and game-based learning may be a way that higher education could combat declining enrollments (Wiggins, 2016).

EFFECTIVENESS OF GAME-BASED LEARNING AND GAMIFICATION

Technological applications have become more common in education today and have triggered some significant changes in education, from kindergarten up to higher education. Classroom instruction is no longer telling for teaching and listening for learning. The digital age has brought about an alternative method of instruction through the use of digital games and multimedia technology. "The ideal learning environment for digital learners are rich learning environments that enable and support learners to learn independently and collaboratively" (Hwa, 2018, p. 259). Classroom instruction has been enhanced by the incorporation of multimedia technology and benefits of digital game-based learning (Hwa, 2018).

Change in Mathematics Learning

The next section of the chapter will focus examples of implementation of game-based learning and gamification in learning environments. Often students have difficulties in learning mathematics in a traditional classroom environment. Students perceive mathematics as being a difficult subject, often evoking feelings of stress, anxiety, and fear. A teacher with an unfriendly attitude and poor presentation skills may worsen the situation, resulting in students losing interest (Hwa, 2018).

As a result, educators are always searching for more efficient and effective ways to improve student learning especially in subjects as important as mathematics. Past studies have indicated that any new skills that young children acquire in a fun, effortless environment enhance their potential to explore the world. Adapting materials using computer-based learning has the potential to provide that motivating learning experience.

The main problem pertaining to children being taught in traditional way of teaching mathematics is the lack of motivation. Children are not motivated because they are not sure how to relate mathematics concepts to everyday life. Learners from elementary school to higher education think of the traditional method of mathematics instruction as "boring" (Hwa, 2018, p. 263). Teachers are now trying to merge the content of learning and the motivation of digital games. Past studies have indicated that motivation is one of the most important parts of learning. The element of "fun" in a game situation will be the key element to motivate current and future learners (Hwa, 2018, p. 264).

Using digital game-based learning, which is user-centered, can promote "challenges, cooperation, engagements, and the development of problem-solving strategies" (Hwa, 2018, p. 264). This design of the learning environment based on the properties of educational games can be the appropriate way to improve learning mathematics. There is extensive empirical evidence which shows a positive effect of the digital games on the students' performance in mathematics and science. One of the most important characteristics of these games is interactivity; therefore, it is crucial that interactivity is embedded in the rules of the game (Hwa, 2018).

Use of Digital Badges in Nursing

A gamification technique such as issuing digital badges has been recognized as the opportunity for personal empowerment. In higher education, digital badges have been explored as "an alternative to grades (micro-credentialing); supporting the progressing through research degrees; assessing individual students in collaborative assignments, and as an introduction to navigating a physical campus through a scavenger hunt exploration" (Garnett & Button, 2018, p. 2).

Digital Badges

Digital badges have been used creatively in higher education; however, nursing education has just begun to explore the usage of badges in microcredentials in hopes of motivating nursing students in clinical performance, an online nursing course, and GPA recognition (Garnett & Button, 2018).

Undergraduate nursing students are required to acquire accurate bioscience knowledge in order to provide "safe evidence based practice" (Garnett & Button, 2018, p. 2). Many of the nursing students have a difficult time consuming the large volume of content and the complex concepts in the topics of bioscience. Digital badges were added to the nursing curriculum to be used as a motivational tool to emphasize the importance of preparing for practical classes. Badges were issued to those who were prepared, indicating the students who were motivated to ensure they were prepared for class (Garnett & Button, 2018).

The physical appearance of digital badges proved to be an important motivating feature. A series of badges were created to be earned for the ten different human systems. Showcasing a badge for each of the ten topics covered each week. Being able to display those ten badges was a huge motivational factor to learn the topic each week. As a result, it was identified that digital badges were the best fit to enhance their learning (Garnett & Button, 2018).

The millennial learners (< 19–24) had a higher interest in playing games than did those 25–30 (Garnett & Button, 2018).

GAMIFICATION IN HUMAN COMPUTATION

Human computation refers to a "general mechanism for using human brain power to solve computational problems" (Wang, Goh, Lim, Vu, & Chua, 2017, p. 814). There are still many "conceptual or perceptual problems that algorithms cannot yet handle" although computing has experienced many advances over the years (Wang et al., 2017, 814). In terms of computation, empirical studies have found that gamification was effective in terms of motivating participation in computational activities (Wang et al., 2017).

Gaming to Teach Factorial Designs

One of the indicators of a successful psychology student is a firm understanding of the principles of research design and methodology. It is believed by the psychology educators that the research methods course is one of the most important for those majoring in psychology. However, students often have a different view of the research methods course.

Often times, students do not appreciate the "real world" and career relevance; thus, they are less motivated to succeed and often have high levels of anxiety about this course. Educators are aware of the difficulty of successfully engaging students in this course. To address this issue, educators have devised many of pedagogical techniques to address the issue (Stansbury & Munro, 2013).

Educators have successfully used videos in the classroom which resulted in improving higher level thinking skills, information and knowledge seeking skills, and core research skills. Lack of student motivation makes it a struggle to teach principles of research design and statistics. According to research, students have reported that playing the Wii Nintendo System helped them to understand the class material, considered it a good class supplement, and made the class more enjoyable (Stansbury & Munro, 2013).

The recent study showed that "integrating video games into a research methods psychology shows a positive impact on students' interest, motivation, and ability to learn factorial design" (Stansbury & Munro, 2013, p. 3). This pedagogical technique improved comprehension of the technique over a lecture-only technique. The findings also indicate that video gaming can be used to address the lack of engagement with the course material in a psychology research methods class. Video gaming can also encourage "exploration, socialization, and creativity" (Stansbury & Munro, 2013, p. 4). Therefore, it might help the students to become better scientific thinkers.

Game Design and Development

In order to prepare the students in a Game Design and Development class, a student-centered approach was used. This method allows students to communicate with classmates while completing gaming design projects according to Damian Ashe, Business Ed instructor at Cheraw High School located in Cheraw, South Carolina (D. Ashe, personal communication, July 11, 2019). This method allows students an opportunity to move around and communicate with classmates as they are completing gaming design projects. This is great for kinesthetic learners.

The class is usually a combination of students with a high programming or gaming knowledge/skill level and several students with learning disabilities, so it is critical to group them properly by deficiency to create the proper learning environment. This approach is important so that students can advance their communication, problem-solving, and critical thinking skills (D. Ashe, personal communication, July 11, 2019).

According to Ashe, students are allowed to view former students' work and power points to review the learning outcomes for the class. Visual countdown timers are used to limit the amount of auditory teaching (10–20 minutes) and to ensure the lesson is covered within the allocated time. Ashe stated that as the instructor, he steps back and allows the students to work on the assignment through collaboration with other classmates and trial and error (D. Ashe, personal communication, July 11, 2019).

According to Ashe, he noticed in his first year of teaching that he lost students after about 15 minutes of lecture; therefore, he found that it is important to create the student-centered approach for instruction. Several of the resources used to teach the class include CodeCombat, Gamemaker, Code.org (Design app/Designing curriculum), and Scratch software for producing games (D. Ashe, personal communication, July 11, 2019).

The aforementioned examples lead to the effectiveness of gamification and game-based learning. The new methods of instruction proved to be effective in various subject areas including math, nursing, psychology, human computation, and game design. The positive impact from the aforementioned pedagogical techniques include improved engagement, exploration, socialization, creativity, motivation, participation, and interactivity. It was also noted that students advanced their communication, problem-solving, and critical thinking skills. As a result, educators are now trying to merge the content of learning and the motivation of digital games.

IMPLEMENTATION IN HIGHER EDUCATION

A decade or so ago, it would have been difficult to find a single course on the topic of gaming and its significance in higher education. Now, it is common to find multiple courses, even entire programs of study around games at community colleges and universities. Although some programs are designed to train the professional game designers, a growing numbers of courses are now using games as an object of study. Today, students are given the opportunity to examine how the role of game shapes culture or how game mechanics support player learning. Games are also used to introduce students to larger ideas and concepts (Holmes & Gee, 2016).

Games are being used to demonstrate principles of learning as well as how they can serve as a hub for distributed teaching and learning systems (Holmes & Gee, 2016). Games are not just an object of study or a focus for professional prep in higher education. Games and their features are being used to "inspire innovations in teaching and learning in higher education," just as they are in K–12 education, the workplace, and the community (Holmes & Gee, 2016, p. 2).

Over recent years, the current state of higher education has been under scrutiny regarding issues such as the rising cost of tuition and the purpose of postsecondary education. One major area of concern is how to utilize new digital technologies to enhance teaching and learning in the most effective way. One way that has been utilized is the Internet. Another has been the creation of different teaching and learning activities.

The traditional "chalk and talk" model of lecture-based instruction that has been around for decades has been challenged. With technology innovations such as the Internet and other digital media, there is more opportunity to add to the existing efforts. With increased pressure from the society, it is now urgent for higher education institutions to search for better ways to take advantage of technology's potential (Holmes & Gee, 2016). The time is now to begin implementing more technology into higher education institutions through educational gaming.

Gamification

Gamification has gained increased attention in education in recent years. It is considered to be a way to improve student engagement, attendance, motivation, and academic performance. The primary focus of gamification is on game mechanics—the building blocks of games. The goal is to use the mechanics to encourage and reward behaviors that support learning and promote social interactions. The purpose is not to design a full-fledged game.

An example would be to design a quest that the student would have to complete in order to show their competence. In an ideal situation, there would be different quests for the students to choose from, depending on interest, allowing them various pathways to reach the same goal (Hung, 2017).

Gamification can also create competitiveness and cooperation. The teams compete for badges, points, or levels. The competition is further emphasized by displaying how the students are ranked on a leaderboard. This allows them to see how they rank in comparison to their classmates. Open Badges may be used to allow students to connect earned badges on professional networks such as LinkedIn, available for potential employers to see (Hung, 2017).

Casey Monette, assistant professor of Education at Coker University in Hartsville, South Carolina, uses gamification primarily as a form for review. Education majors at the Wiggins School of Education use gamification to help them practice skills and to review concepts and skills. Professor Monette uses it in the form of Kahoot, Quizziz, and digital breakouts (C. Monette, personal communication, July 2, 2019).

Student Teams

Professor Monette's sessions have been successful because the students are driven by competition and achievement. In the digital breakout sessions, the students have to work together as a team in order to move to the next task. The students have to problem-solve and collaborate in order to complete the task. The student cannot move to the next task until they get the task correct. Game elements including scenarios, sound effects, and timer help the students to focus and challenge them to achieve the goal of completing the digital breakout, thus applying their learning and skill knowledge (C. Monette, personal communication, July 2, 2019).

> Professor Monette feels using gamification in university courses can be beneficial to get students to apply their learning and skill knowledge in an engaging way. Instead of question and answer sessions or discussions, gamification can help get all students engaged in the course content and skills and allows all students to be held accountable. Also, professors can get data on students' performance so that he/she can modify instruction and/or meet with students as needed. (C. Monette, personal communication, July 2, 2019)

Game-Based Learning

Game-based learning is a type of digital game play with defined learning outcomes. Games for entertainment have been used to motivate learners to stay engaged through a series of game features that are of a motivational nature. The features could include incentive structures such as points, badges, stars, or trophies for completion of specific activities (Plass, Homer, & Kinzer, 2015). Another reason to consider digital games for learning is that they allow numerous ways to engage learners.

Learner Engagement

The type of engagement (affective, cognitive, behavioral, sociocultural) to be implemented depends on the decision that would reflect the learning goal, learner characteristics, and the setting. The learner engagement is facilitated by ways of making the game adaptive depending on the situation. This may involve modification of the type problem or the use of scaffolding in a way to respond to the player's in-game actions. Another argument for game-based learning is that it allows graceful failure. It is not thought to be an undesirable outcome, but to sometimes be expected as a necessary step in the learning process (Plass et al., 2015).

An Example

Joshua Bastean, assistant professor of Coker University, Hartsville, South Carolina, created an alternative reality game (ARG) for his Honors ELA students to play in order to teach research and 21st-century skills, as well as a variety of cross-curricular content. The premise for the activity was a zombie apocalypse caused by a virus that affected anyone over the age of 18. Students were put in charge of the school and tasked with overcoming problems brought about by this undead plague. The students would provide a daily report of what they had chosen to do in each situation, supported by research.

If the research was good (e.g., credible sources, proper MLA formatting, and findings that supported their decision), they received a positive outcome to the problem. Otherwise, they received a negative outcome. There were more facets to the project especially as it continued and each class solved problems in unique ways (J. Bastean, personal communication, July 2, 2019).

Professor Bastean states that he has used this activity in high school classes and also at the university. He feels that using an ARG in higher education is more successful than in high school due to having more freedom. He feels college students have more free time as well as more agency over their free time. College students are usually much more mature and can work more effectively in teams (J. Bastean, personal communication, July 2, 2019).

Elements of Game Design for Learning

Although there are many definitions of a game, most follow the four building blocks:

- Game mechanics: the essential game play description—the learning focus activities that are repeated by the learner throughout the game.
- Visual aesthetic design: includes the visual elements such as the look and feel of the game and the characters, including the key information in the game.
- Narrative design: the storyline that is advanced through features such as in-game actions, dialogue, and voice-overs.
- Incentive system: includes the motivational elements that aim to encourage players to continue their efforts and feedback that may modify their behavior.
- Musical store: provides background sounds; often used to direct the attention of the player to specific events or moments in a game.
- Content and skills: the subject matter content and the skills the game is designed to teach. When considering the content, it may be useful to the four functions of games:
  - Preparation of future learning: does not have own learning objective, but provides students with shared experiences, for example, class discussions.
  - Teaching new knowledge and skills: introduction of new skills and knowledge for the learner to acquire as part of the game.
  - Practice and reinforce existing knowledge and skills: provides opportunities to practice existing knowledge; basic cognitive skills.
  - Developing 21st-century skills: provides opportunities to develop more complex socioemotional skills related to teamwork, collaboration, problem-solving, and communication (Plass et al., 2015, p. 264).

While it is difficult to define the learning goals for a term as broad as game, the items above capture many of the subgenres of games. It is noted that not all learning needs require the use of all of these elements (Plass et al., 2015).

Digital games have not always inspired students in higher education. According to some students in Singapore who were found to have a high level of intrinsic motivation, they showed no increase in motivation or engagement as a result of game usage. Further assessments relating to student learning indicated the continued need of the lecture with digital learning combination (Turner, Johnston, Kebritchi, Evans, & Heflich, 2018).

STUDENT ATTRACTION TO GAMIFICATION AND GAME-BASED LEARNING

Motivation, the "holy grail" of education is so important, but little is known about what it will take to motivate students (Ark & Wise, 2011, p. 76). Because of the need for students to work hard, it is important that educators know what captures their attention and aids them to persist through discomfort and distraction. It is important to know the intrinsic and extrinsic factors that together bring out a student's behavior, "a personal motivational profile" that will change the education profession (Ark & Wise, 2011, p. 76).

Researchers are getting very close to making this reality and game designers are the ones to thank. A lot can be learned about behaviors by observations to the casual game space. The different games attract the different players. Some of the preferences include combat, collaboration, realism, alternative, and exploration. Games also offer the benefit of public victories and private failures, both of which are important to students (Ark & Wise, 2011).

Educators can learn something about engagement, commitment, and motivation from the gaming world. Tom Chatfield, author of *Fun, Inc.*, considers himself a game theorist and is interested in how games draw on the pleasure centers to improve the world, including educating children. He has identified seven factors indicating how games can be used to motivate learning. The seven factors include:

- Continuous grading: participants have the ability to watch their progression.
- Multiple long- and short-term aims that are clearly defined: it is always clear in a game what the aims are, but that does not mean that they are always simple; they could exist on multiple fronts and reward multiple forms of success.
- Rewarding effort: in most games, the player gets credit every time something is done. Engagement helps with progression. Never punished for failure; only rewarded for trying and for success.
- Feedback: immediate and continuous feedback. Gamers can fail in millions of small ways, learn what to change, and move on.
- Element of uncertainty: surprising experiences and rewards, pitched at the right level of uncertainty so the gamer does not get bored. The experiences surprise enough to create high engagement.
- Finding windows of learning: moments of engagement points when learning is taking place; best to give people something to remember.
- Confidence: result is not just enhanced learning, but confidence. The reward system of gaming makes people braver, willing to take risks, and harder to discourage (Ark & Wise, 2011, 51, 52).

These seven factors would likely not come as a surprise to most experienced and effective educators; however, they would likely be the first to say that trying to apply these factors to the classroom is difficult. "The new generation of computer games are adaptive, able to adjust the level of difficulty to the player, finding students' instructional levels where they learn best, and offering just enough of a challenge to get them learning" (Ark & Wise, 2011, p. 81).

The traditional pedagogy models for higher education are becoming more ineffective as well as challenging to apply to the traditional classroom. Educators are finding it difficult to motivate students to complete readings, assignments, and participate in classroom discussions. Students are finding it difficult to participate in any activities that do not provide direct assessment. Motivation is an issue with students and was stated as a contributing factor (63%) as a reason for student withdrawal (Hitchens & Tulloch, 2018, p. 28).

Challenge

There is a great challenge for higher education pedagogy as well as an opportunity. The issue will not lie with the educator nor with the syllabi. The issue is a reflection of the generational change in the way that people learn. Many students today have spent their school years learning through "video games, online environments, and social networks" and rather than breaking them from the habit, this is the time "to embrace the pedagogic potential of these systems" (Hitchens & Tulloch, 2018, p. 29).

If the gaming logistics and mechanisms can be adapted and applied to the classroom environment, it will be easier for the educators to develop new methods of pedagogy that will engage and appeal to the contemporary and future students (Hitchens & Tulloch, 2018). As stated by Professor Monette, "gamification is common to students and a part of their everyday lives. Students are used to playing games; therefore, using these game components can help them learn and apply the course content in a more engaging way" (C. Monette, personal communication, July 2, 2019).

The importance of motivation has been emphasized in gamification; however, this does not indicate that an educator will be able to take an aspect of a game and apply it to a non-game context and the student will be instantly motivated in the way the educator intended. Based on research, three principles for "evaluating whether an element might be successful used in gamification, are based on intrinsic motivation: relatedness, competence, and autonomy" (Hitchens & Tulloch, 2018, p. 31).

These three elements can be used to judge whether a game-design element will be useful in providing the needed motivation. Previous research indicates that students need a positive mental attitude for effective learning. Without this, no classroom approach will be successful.

"Being digital natives, millennium students need a different learning approach which can engage their inquisitive minds; and the conventional teaching and learning approaches used in the classrooms do not work and need to be replaced" (Hwa, 2018, p. 264).

GAMIFICATION AND GAME-BASED LEARNING IN THE 21ST CENTURY

Although teachers are continuously searching for new instructional approaches, it is agreed that schools today are facing major problems around student engagement and motivation. The use of educational games as learning tools has the potential to be a positive approach due to the ability to teach and reinforce skills. The use of games teaches other important skills such as collaboration, problem-solving, and communication.

They can also be used as a great motivational tool. Developing an engaging, full-blown instructional game is, however, time consuming, difficult, and costly. Therefore, many instructors will choose not to implement them into their classrooms for these reasons. As opposed to using elaborate games requiring a lot of developing efforts, the gamification approach is suggested using only game-thinking and game-design elements to improve motivation and engagement (Dicheva, Dichev, Agre, & Angelova, 2015).

Graduation Levels

According to research, 75% of nontraditional or adult learners enroll in college in the United States; however, only 33.7% graduate with a degree or certificate. On the other hand, 60.7% of traditional learners graduated. It is critical to academic success and the continuing workforce that an instructional strategy is found that will engage, motivate, and retain nontraditional students.

Digital game-based education (a combination of educational content with videos) has shown promise in adult education and learning (Turner et al., 2018). The games are designed for educational purposes and to engage the diverse learning styles. Game-based education has shown to increase cognitive abilities such as perception, reasoning, critical thinking, and memory retention (Turner et al., 2018).

The use of digital game-based learning is in the early stages of development in community colleges and universities due to the insufficient data regarding learning outcomes and assessments that are linked to digital game-based learning; however, the technology-savvy students seek an interactive, hands-on learning experience that is available in the digital game-based learning curriculum. In order to increase the teacher effectiveness, instructors must develop an internal understanding of the structure of digital game design as well as the limitations of technology (Turner et al., 2018).

With the increased broadband of online communities, the use of digital games present a new set of engaging tools and techniques based on the mechanics such as competition, missions, and quests. Digital educational games seek to inform, educate, and motivate learners. Digital education games are also helping to extend the range of ability to learn in the classroom by making the world the classroom and putting social interactions at the center of the learning experience rather than curriculum (Whitton, 2014).

Professor Basten believes that technology will only serve to enhance using alternate reality games in teaching. Students and teachers will have access to more information than those with technology. In addition, "communication will be more effective if they choose to use technologies such as Slack, Google Hangouts, or other instant messaging services. As he looks further into the 21st century, he believes that the only limits are the instructor's and the student's imaginations" (J. Basten, personal communication, July 2, 2019).

CONCLUSION

It is believed that the five key emerging trends in gaming will be the following:

1. Mobile gaming using GPS
2. Social interaction
3. Casual play with short learning curves
4. Short engagements
5. Use of radical interfaces such as motion control (Whitton, 2014, p. 190).

It is also anticipated that there will be three emerging trends in game-based learning:

- The current hype over gamification will die down, as it is shown not to be a motivational panacea.
- The market will become more saturated with badges, points, and leaderboards.
- A gradual shift to more sophisticated models of gamification, perhaps "playification." Exploration and creation, curiosity fulfillment, and exploration of play rather than extrinsic motivators (Whitton, 2014, p. 190).

With technology changing so rapidly, it is never too late to begin planning for the next phase of innovations and what will be the new wave of the future.

CHAPTER SUMMARY

- The use of games in academics is a relatively new concept.
- Games can make learning more fun for students as well as provide an opportunity for creative thinking.
- Game-based learning and gamification are two different concepts.
- When students are given the opportunity to enter in a state of playing, their level of concentration tends to rise higher than normal.
- Gamification and game-based learning may be ways that higher education can combat declining enrollments.
- Students are not motivated to learn mathematics because they do not see how math relates to everyday life.
- There has been extensive empirical evidence showing a positive effect of digital games on performance in math and science.
- In higher education, digital badges have been explored as an alternative to grades.
- The physical appearance of digital badges proved to be an important motivating feature to learning.
- In terms of computation, empirical studies have found that gamification was effective in terms of motivating participation in computational activities.
- According to research with students studying psychology, those playing the Wii helped them to understand the class material and made the class more enjoyable.
- Educators are trying to merge the content of learning and the motivation of digital games.
- Gamification has gained increased attention in education in recent years.
- Educators can learn something about engagement, commitment, and motivation from the gaming world.
- Tom Chatfield, author of *Fun, Inc.*, considers himself a game theorist and is interested in how games draw on pleasure centers to improve the world, including educating children.
- If gaming logistics and mechanisms can be adapted and applied to the classroom environment, it will be easier for the educators to develop new methods of pedagogy that will engage and appeal to contemporary and future students.

NOTE

1. Editor's Note: Gaming is a method that has the potential to become a recognized and highly useful pedagogy in the 21st century because of its motivational ability. It is a teaching method well worth the effort to learn and use in the instructional process.

REFERENCES

Al-Azawi, R., Al-Faliti, F., & Al-Blushi, M. (2016, August). Educational gamification vs. game based learning: Comparative study. *International Journal of Innovation, Management and Technology, 7*, 132–135. https://doi.org/10.18178/ijimt.2016.7.4.659.

Ark, T. V., & Wise, B. (2011). *Getting smart: How digital learning is changing the world*. Retrieved from https://search-proquest-com.proxy200.nclive.org/central/docview/2130990897/bookReader?accountid=15065.

Dicheva, D., Dichev, C., Agre, G., & Angelova, G. (2015). Gamification in education: A systematic mapping study. *Educational Technology & Society, 18*(3), 1–14. Retrieved from https://search-proquest.com.proxy.

Garnett, T., & Button, D. (2018). The use of digital badges by undergraduate nursing students: A three-year study. *Nurses Education in Practice, 32*, 1–8. https://doi.org/10.1016/j.nepr.2018.06.013.

Hitchens, M., & Tulloch, R. (2018). A gamification design for the classroom. *Interactive Technology and Smart Education, 15*(1), 28. Retrieved from https://search-proquest-com.proxy200.nclive.org.

Holmes, J. B., & Gee, E. R. (2016). A framework for understanding game-based teaching and learning. *On The Horizon, 24*(1–16), 1–16. https://doi.org/10.

Hung, A. C. (2017). A critique and defense of gamification. *Journal of Interactive Online Learning, 15*, 57–69. Retrieved from www.ncolr.org/jiol.

Hwa, S. P. (2018). Pedagogical change in mathematics learning: Harnessing the power of digital game-based learning. *Educational Technology & Society, 21*, 259–276.

Plass, J. L., Homer, B. D., & Kinzer, C. K. (2015). Foundations of game-based learning. *Educational Psychologist, 50*, 258–283. https://doi.org/10.1080/00461520.2015.1122533.

Stansbury, J. A., & Munro, G. D. (2013). Gaming in the classroom: An innovative way to teach factorial designs. *Teaching of Psychology*. https://doi.org/10.1177/0098628312475037.

Turner, P. E., Johnston, E., Kebritchi, M., Evans, S., & Heflich, D. A. (2018). Influence of online computer games on the academic achievement on nontraditional undergraduate students. *Cogent Education*, 1–16. https://doi.org/10.1080/2331186X.2018.1437671.

Wang, X., Goh, D. H., Lim, E., Vu, A. W., & Chua, A. Y. (2017). Examining the effectiveness of gamification in human computation. *International Journal of Human-Computer Interaction, 33*, 813–821. https://doi.org/10.1080/10447318.2017.1287458.

Whitton, N. (2014). *Digital games and learning: Research and theory*. New York, NY: Routledge.

Wiggins, B. E. (2016, January–March). An overview and study on the use of games, simulations, and gamification in higher education. *International Journal of Game-Based Learning, 6*, 18–28. https://doi.org/10.4018/IJGBL.2016010102.

Chapter 6

YouTube Education[1]

Antonio Jefferson

BACKGROUND

YouTube was launched in 2005, founded by Jawed Kari, Steve Chen, and Chad Hurley. As employees of PayPal, the three came to the realization that there was not a central location on the Internet to upload and view videos. In February of that year the domain name was registered and in April, the first ever video was uploaded to the site (Ace, 216).

After being purchased by Google, YouTube saw their biggest advancements in 2009. The site launched full HD videos, developed a partnership to deliver catch-up TV, and boosted approximately 1 billion views per day. In addition, YouTube found that users were also using the site for gaming and blogging which increased popularity even more (Ace, 2016).

Since YouTube's inception in 2005, it has continued to grow and develop. The site is now home to a multibillion-dollar company that more than 1.3 billion people visit daily and more than 300 hours of video are uploaded each minute (Ace, 2016). YouTube in classrooms and other academic formats has also become an important use for the site.

From walking students through word problems to implementing a TEDx Talk for a lesson, the site has increasingly become a vital tool for educators. To provide better insight into how popular and useful YouTube has become in academia, this chapter will highlight specifically how the site is currently being implement in lesson plans in elementary, secondary, community college, and universities.

Elementary Schools

There are four main areas that elementary schools use YouTube to enhance instruction and overall learning outcomes. These methods allow students to form thoughts, experiences, and demonstrations. In addition, YouTube provides the visual and sound element that will easily keep students' attention (Catapano, 2018).

The four methods include the following:

A) Flipped Instruction: YouTube videos provide the opportunity to learn more about a lesson prior to it being introduced inside the classroom. In addition, this method allows for group work outside the classroom in an interactive way (Catapano, 2018).
B) Supplemental Information: If additional information is required to complete a lesson or a teacher has run out of time, YouTube links can be assigned to further a discussion or lesson plan (Catapano, 2018).
C) Self-Directed Learning: Part of lesson plan can direct students to use YouTube as a resource for an assignment. The opportunity to use YouTube will help them learn how to work independently or learn more about a specific passion (Catapano, 2018).
D) Classroom Enhancement: Videos are more engaging and provides more diverse learning techniques than other methods such as textbooks or pictures. The free resource can also be used as a space filler by using music in between class lessons (Catapano, 2018).

In interviewing a current kindergarten teacher from Sumter, South Carolina, the author had the opportunity to get more insight into positive teaching methods and challenges with using YouTube in her classroom. She explained that she uses YouTube in the following ways: to help students read out loud, to learn songs, to learn letter recognition and sounds, to develop research projects, to work on small group assignments, to create a class YouTube channel, and to write opinion texts (L Burns, personal communication, July 12, 2019). She explained:

> Sometimes I have to make sure students do not click on anything inappropriate when working in a small group. My assistant and I monitor the small groups, but sometimes it is difficult to go from one group to another, making sure they stay on task. Access is also a challenge that we face at times. Videos at school may not be accessible at home. Which can cause some students to get behind on their lesson. (L. Burns, personal communication, July 12, 2019)

Overall, she believes that YouTube is a great resource in the classroom. She has seen numerous benefits such as students having the ability to listen to other students read and access to different parts of the world for cultural lesson plans. In addition, she believes the future impact for YouTube in the classroom stretches far beyond the imagination. "I look forward to the day where I will have students from around the world in my classroom at the same time, with just the click of a button" (J. Smith, personal communication, July 12, 2019).

Community Colleges

The community college system has also seen an increase in using YouTube as a teaching method. With the rise of online and hybrid courses, community colleges are becoming innovative in the ways that instructors use technology in the classroom. In an interview with a communications instructor at a community college in rural, North Carolina, she boosted about the positive impact she has with using YouTube in her lesson plans.

She explained, "YouTube is utilized to complement the lessons in my classroom. For instance, when I review particular speeches for public speaking, the students watch and critique speeches on YouTube for a better understanding of the assignment and how a speech should be prepared and delivered" (L. Matthews, personal communication, July 14, 2019).

She went on to highlight that one of the biggest benefits of using YouTube as a teaching method is because it provides students with an extra resource that can be implemented to boost confidence. The ability to easily navigate the site also adds to a benefit inside the classroom.

Although YouTube is a reliable source to assist in teaching, it does come with challenges. The instructor noted that on some occasions when she has gone through a lesson and assigned a YouTube link as for an assignment, without knowledge the videos have been removed (L. Mathews, personal communication, July 14, 2019). It often means that she has to come up with an alternative at the last minute. Even though that may be a minor glitch, she believes YouTube will continue to expand in other areas of higher education.

She responded that "I believe YouTube will also be used for marketing purposes in the future. With community college enrollment decreasing, YouTube would be a way to promote academic objectives in a cost-effective way so enrollment may increase" (L. Mathews, personal communication, July 14, 2019).

Four-Year Colleges and Universities

Four-year colleges and universities have also shown a continued growth in implementing YouTube in the course curriculum. In an interview with an adjunct instructor from the University of North Carolina at Charlotte (UNCC), she provided details on ways she has used YouTube in the classroom.

She informed the interviewer that "I look for videos that break down the topic being discussed in a way that provides a different stimulant for students to engage in the material" (A. Smith, personal communication, July 15, 2019). Similar to the use of YouTube in elementary school classrooms, the instructor from UNCC explained the diversity YouTube brings in the classroom.

> I think it benefits my teaching method because, it provides validity to what I as the instructors am sharing or vice versa. Many students like to see videos, so that gives them an experience of diverse teaching methods. It opens up the minds of the students I teach to think about the variety of ways in which they can communicate with each other. It also provides critical discussion what was good or what could have been improved about the YouTube video. I definitely see YouTube being the standard in classrooms in the future. Because technology is so ingrained in our society, I see YouTube continuing to build upon detailed ways in how people learn. (A. Smith, personal communication, July 15, 2019)

YouTube in Saudi Arabia

YouTube has been successful in numerous academic forms in both secondary and higher education sectors. The online sharing website provides an opportunity for students to use interactive techniques to help students learn materials.

In Saudi Arabia, students use YouTube technology in an English as a Foreign Language (EFL) course. The course aims at developing certain observation skills for teaching in elementary schools (Alwehaibi, 2015). The study divided students into two groups, in which one group used the support of YouTube for instruction and one did not. Both groups studied a course titled "Observation in Schools." The experimental group used YouTube videos about classroom presentations, PowerPoints, and other online media. The control group was taught the same content, only they used the traditional lecture-based method (Alwehaibi, 2015).

Comparative Results

The results of the study found that YouTube as a teaching method had a significant positive impact on EFL students enrolled in the course (Alwehibi, 2015). The study highlights that YouTube creates an enjoyable, entertaining learning atmosphere that makes retaining information easier. In addition, the study revealed that students in the experimental group were highly motivated to watch, read, discuss, and take part in various activated as a result of the YouTube learning process (Alwehaibi, 2015).

Another approach for using YouTube as a successful teaching method was used in a college psychology course. The study used *Blended Learning*

Theory and Information Processing Theory to successfully introduce technology into the classroom (Fleck, Beckman, Sterns, & Hussey, 2014). The study took 85 psychology students from a large, urban, community college enrolled in various sections of Developmental Education Psychology (Fleck et al., 2014). Throughout the semester, prior to attending class, participants completed the assigned textbook reading and took a quiz online.

At the beginning of each in-class session, students were able to watch a YouTube clip that correlated with the assigned chapter. After that portion of the lesson plan was completed, the class proceeded with traditional lectures and in-class activities. On the last day of class students completed a post-semester survey that reflected using YouTube as a teaching method (Fleck et al., 2014).

Results found that 68 students indicated that YouTube was helpful for the course and a successful approach for academics in general. Seven students concluded that YouTube did not help in the course. Overall, nearly all 85 students found that YouTube clips were enjoyable and a positive teaching method (Fleck et al., 2014).

USES OF YOUTUBE

Oral Presentations

YouTube is also evolving as a way to assign oral presentations in the classroom. As technology continues to advance, the days of face-to-face boardroom meetings are becoming obsolete. Meetings are now taking place on software such as Zoom, FaceTime, and Skype. The ability to articulate and present through these sites is becoming increasingly vital for professional development.

A research study out of the University of New England in Arimdale, Australia, examined how students would respond to an assignment of giving an oral presentation on YouTube. Oral presentations on YouTube are noted to having the following advantages: more conducive for large classes or online courses, saves class time, allows students to view their own performance, allows easier grading, and provides the opportunity to assess behaviors (Malouff & Emmenon, 2015).

To measure the effectiveness of using YouTube for oral presentations, 162 students enrolled in a Behavior Modification Psychology course were asked to record themselves describing how to apply behavior modification principles to change a specific type of behavior. The two main goals of the assignment were to increase skill and confidence in public speaking and improve their knowledge of the topic (Malouff & Emmenon, 2015).

A self-evaluation was a second component of the assignment that asked students to evaluate themselves on items ranging from how loud they spoke in the oral presentation and their eye contact. Results found that almost every student submitted an oral presentation on YouTube and 48 students completed the self-evaluation. Overall feedback indicated that students viewed the YouTube oral presentation experience as positive and helped to increase presentation skills (Malouff & Emmenon, 2015).

Online Courses

As technology continues to evolve and regularly become integrated in education, online courses are gaining the interest of students. Online courses allow students to be flexible with their time and other obligations such as a full-time job. In addition, it decreases the price tag of higher education. Students enrolled in online courses do not carry the burden of room or board or other fee typically encountered by residential students.

With the growing popularity of online classes, instructors are also using YouTube videos to guide lesson plans and as a teaching method. The reasons to use YouTube in online classes include (A) Unlimited Content, (B) Ideal for Mobile Learning, and (C) Easy to Integrate (Batchelor, 2016).

An online course was developed to measure how students could effectively communicate through an online class using Blackboard as the course management system. The course titled "Technology, Innovation and Organization Change" assigned students the roles of CEOs and charged them with delivering a speech to a group of executives. Each student was assigned to write, deliver, and record an 8–10-minute speech with a webcam, then upload the video onto YouTube and embed the video within a thread on the Blackboard discussion board (Batchelor, 2016).

Results of Using Webcams and YouTube

Results found that the introduction of technology such as webcams and YouTube produced a positive reaction from students. Even though some students found the process of recording themselves and embedding it into the online discussion a bit stressful, the learning curve did assist them in other online courses (Batchelor, 2016).

The instructor believed that introducing video into online classes is innovative because it offers instructors and online students some of the same advantages of seated courses. In addition, the use of web cameras and YouTube activities gives students a chance to meet one another and provide feedback (Batchelor, 2016). The use of YouTube in online courses will continue to evolve as all education levels begin to introduce hybrid and online classes for students.

Teaching Method

YouTube encompasses a wide range of benefits in the classroom and in online courses. Implementing YouTube videos into course curriculum allows students to receive diverse perspectives on lessons, receive feedback through assignments, and discuss a lesson at home. The following strategies and techniques highlight why YouTube is an effective teaching method in higher education.

Diverse Unlimited Content

YouTube provides access to almost unlimited content. As almost 400 hours are uploaded every minute, instructors have a wide range of videos to help guide lessons or assign work. In addition, the organization of YouTube videos is user friendly for both students and instructors. The site contains a reach source of micro lectures, online tutorials, how-to videos, TEDx Talks (Batchelor, 2016).

Mobile Learning

Cellphones and other handheld devices have changed dramatically in the few years. Individuals are able to shop, play games, or video chat with someone around the world at the touch of a button. It is also likely that students will be using mobile devices to watch course content. The compatibility of YouTube allows for seamless mobile transition for online students. Recent figures show that more than half of YouTube views come from handheld devices, which makes it even more essential for instructors to implement YouTube as a teaching method (Batchelor, 2016).

Easy Integration

Commonly used e-learn software includes systems such as Canvas and Blackboard. These systems allow course content to be uploaded. Students can interact through discussion board features and even video chat (Batchelor, 2016). The flexibility of YouTube allows instructors to upload, embed, and share videos within the online class.

Multimedia in the Classroom

Instructors are continuing to advance their use of multimedia in the classroom, due to expectations in the use of technology for current students. The ability to implement YouTube videos in class allows students to work and maintain attention on a concept throughout the duration of the video (Fleck et al., 2014). For instance, a concept can be introduced in a lecture; the instructor can later assign a YouTube clip that reinforces the concept introduced in the class. The YouTube video can potentially add additional factors. Other benefits of introducing multimedia in the classroom include the availability of diverse materials and relevance to target populations (Fleck et al., 2014).

Increased Discussions

Classroom discussions are a general practice in disciplines from literature courses to history classes. Discussions insist that students are engaged and active in the conversations (Fleck et al., 2014). Introducing YouTube videos into classroom discussions allow students to hear diverse perspectives and provide the opportunity to continue dialogue after class.

Skill Development and Application

As students expand their knowledge and critical thinking ability, they develop a better understanding of how to draw from different concepts and ideas to solve problems (Fleck et al., 2014). Multimedia tools such as YouTube videos provide an opportunity to expand the understanding of a topic and provide diverse context to the issue (Fleck et al., 2014). For example, if students in a Biology class are exposed to techniques on dissection through YouTube video media, the exposure increases the understanding of dissection. This specific skill development is enhanced through exposure of YouTube videos in the classroom.

Diversity and Learning Needs

Textbooks and other outdated teaching materials can lack the diversity that is present in the current student population or college community. This challenge places the responsibility of instructors to introduce diverse perspectives in the classroom or online courses. YouTube is a great resource that will help instructors provide cultural context to relevant issues in society or lesson plan (Fleck et al., 2014).

For example, when introducing the Civil Rights Movement of the 1960s into a history course, YouTube videos can be instrumental in introducing actual footage and personal narratives from individuals who participated in the movement. This method is more engaging and adds value to the lesson unlike the passages in a textbook (Fleck et al., 2014).

Availability of Material

Instructors have access to endless lesson materials with the use of YouTube as an instruction tool. From speeches to historical videos, educators can implement a YouTube video in almost any lesson plan. One of the most utilized and effective videos for educators are instructional videos (Fleck et al., 2014). In addition to YouTube assignments for students, educators also find benefits from using YouTube. There are multiple channels dedicated to supporting instructors in art, political science, math, history, and foreign languages (Fleck et al., 2014). These channels offer teaching tips, lesson plan management, and multimedia integration ideas for educators.

Attention and Memory

Instructors can present information in numerous ways. It is essential for instructors to consider the various ways in which students can learn from their teaching style and peers. The Information Processing Theory explains that, to create memory, individuals are exposed to information via sensory input that is either visual or audio (Fleck et al., 2014). The Information Processing Theory is one that instructors should really lean on as they prepare lesson plans.

YouTube videos can serve as a teaching resource to serve both of those purposes. For example, if students are enrolled in a literature class and the topic of discussion is on interpreting the writings of an author, the student can use YouTube videos to guide their thoughts based on available content.

Peer Discussions

Similar to using multimedia such as YouTube to facilitate learning goals and homework assignments, YouTube is also beneficial for peer discussions in the classroom. There have been numerous studies that highlight the importance of interaction among peers in a classroom environment (Fleck et al., 2014). For example, a structured classroom debate allows students to lead, strategize, and work within a team around a specific topic. The activity allows students to work together and learn from each other in the process. YouTube videos in peer discussions allow learning to be transformed from passive to active and inclusive (Fleck et al., 2014).

HIGHER EDUCATION IN THE 21ST CENTURY

As technology continues to advance, so will the expectations of students at colleges and universities. In some public schools, students already have access to Chromebooks and iPads in the classroom in first grade. They are surrounded by technology in all aspects of life. Once students enter higher education, they are already accustomed to using YouTube, Blackboard, Zoom, and other online resources. To continue in development, faculty also need to implement these forms of technology in the classroom for students.

It is also vital to embrace technology in the classroom because it will prepare students for future employment opportunities. The future is full of technology advancements, such as fully automated vehicles, fully functional robots, and additive manufacturing (Staat, 2019). To ensure that students are prepared to major in career fields such as engineering or information technology, there needs to be continuous exposure to technology at all levels of education. Using YouTube as a teaching method in the classroom is a basic approach for instructors to use for success.

YouTube and Campus Libraries

Miami Dade College, located in Miami Florida, enrolls one of the largest student bodies in the country. The college is home to eight campuses and one education center. In 2013, Miami Dade College was recognized as having the largest enrollment of any college or university in the country. In the 2014–15 academic year, the college enrolled 92,085 credit earning students (Miami Dade College, 2019).

Miami Dade College's eight libraries are designed to meet the academic needs of all faculty, staff, and students. Serving as the center piece for academic teaching resources, training, and community programs, multimedia tools such as YouTube play a significant role in decimating information to individuals. In addition to YouTube serving as a resource, Miami Dade College also uniquely offers a one credit literacy information course. The course aims to help students, faculty, and staff develop foundational library search practices and access reliable sources provided by the library (Miami Dade College, 2019).

While interviewing one of the associate directors of Learning Resources, she was able to provide insight on how the Miami Dade College library uses YouTube for campus support. She explained, "Our library uses YouTube to support faculty in the classroom by keeping the videos on reserve for students to review when needed" (A. Gaddis, personal communication, July 18, 2019).

She was also able to provide the benefits of using YouTube as a library resource. She noted,

> I think the benefits are that students can always have access to vital information, without having to physically step foot in the library. They are able to log on from any location to get the information they need. I also believe that a huge benefit is that YouTube is a platform that students are already comfortable with using, so we do not have to spend time teaching them how to navigate, which makes them more confident in their abilities. (A. Gaddis, personal communication July 18, 2019)

Although library administrators have found the use of YouTube beneficial and easy to navigate, there have been some challenges in implementing the resource. The Miami Dade library administrator explained,

> I think a lot of the challenges with using YouTube comes from the academic side of the college. Some faculty are not familiar with how to upload content on YouTube, so they stray away from using it, even though we see how effective it for learning. Also, some faculty refuse to use YouTube because they do not want their classroom content available outside the walls of the classroom. (A. Gaddis, personal communication July 18, 2019)

As technology and YouTube continues to evolve, she believes there will be endless opportunities for the resource in the library. She explained, "I see the use of YouTube being further integrated in the library, similar to the way we are able to house textbooks for course reserves. It is a big benefit for the library on the digital side as we all move in that direction" (A. Gaddis, personal communication July 18, 2019).

YouTube for Educators

YouTube EDU is a subsection of YouTube that provides access to over 500,000 educational videos from institutions like Stanford University and organization like, PBS, TED, Khan Academy, and Steve Spangler Science. The videos are grouped in the following categories: primary education, secondary education, life-long learning, and reflecting academic discipline. These categories allow educators to view videos in order to develop lesson plans and group activities or prepare for a new subject (YouTube for Educators, 2019).

YouTube Teacher

YouTube Teacher is a site that shows teachers how to use YouTube in the classroom. The ability to create your own videos provides the following: eliminates ads, builds personal instructor videos, and recommends other teacher's videos. This site is dedicated specifically for teachers because they use YouTube for a unique reason. Although most are using YouTube for entertainment purposes, teachers are using it to develop course lessons, learning outcomes, and teambuilding. The opportunity to have all those videos in one location provides seamless integrations (YouTube for Educators, 2019).

Pedagogical Benefits

Research has shown that the concept of teaching by implementing videos in the classroom curriculum is beneficial. The idea of a flipped classroom is described as learners having the ability to digest lecture content at their own pace (Pedagogical Benefits, 2019). The evolution of YouTube has continued to innovate this teaching style through mobile capabilities and other technology advancements. The following highlights benefits of a flipped classroom for educators and students.

- Facilitating thinking and problem solving: The creative challenge of using moving images enables learners to acquire a range of transferable skill (Pedagogical Benefits, 2019).
- Assisting with mastery learning: Videos can be used as an instructor in communicating facts. Students can view instructional videos or complex clinicals for skill development (Pedagogical Benefits, 2019).
- Inspiring and engaging students: Videos implemented in class discussions have been proven to increase student motivations, enhance learning experiences, higher grades and better team learning opportunities (Pedagogical Benefits, 2019).
- Authentic learning: Videos encourage academic rigor and the ability to apply critical thinking skills in numerous situations (Pedagogical Benefits, 2019).

WINGATE UNIVERSITY

Wingate University in Wingate, North Carolina, uses YouTube in a course titled, First Year Experience (FYE). It uses TEDx Talks found on YouTube to motivate students, assist in navigating challenges that they may encounter as a first-generation student and how to academically prepare for their new level of education. In a course titled "Race and Sports," YouTube videos were instrumental in comparing how sports and race was viewed in the 1930s and 1940s versus today. The opportunity to view documentaries and hear personal narrative added a sense of value to the topics being learned.

YouTube has also made assignments more engaging for students. Reading articles and books can often be challenging for students grasp or find interest. However, assigning YouTube videos, along with a written assignment, helped students learn more about navigating different forms of technology and helped them take a more directive approach to learning. There was always positive feedback when the instructor attached a YouTube video to any assignment.

YouTube has made teaching a smoother transition for individuals who do not have extensive experience in the classroom or in a specific subject. YouTube allows instructors to fill in gaps with experts or make classroom activities more engaging. In addition, YouTube's instructional videos provided a sense of confidence in the role as instructor. YouTube provided videos on teambuilders, ice breakers, and other group activities to help ease the transition of a new class. The tools and insight provided by YouTube is a very valuable resource.

CONCLUSION

Technology has dramatically changed daily lives. Individuals can shop for groceries, clothes, and household supplies without leaving the comfort of their homes. Individuals can connect with someone at the click of a button through social media sites such as Facebook and Twitter. Board meetings will never be the same, as virtual meetings through sites such as Zoom and Skype provide new possibilities.

Higher education is now moving into embracing technology in the classroom, with an understanding that it is preparing students for the workforce of the future. In conducting several interviews with educators at all levels, it was found that students are already entering with expectations of using the latest technology as a resource and teaching tool. The benefits of implementing YouTube into course lessons are many. In elementary school, students are using YouTube to learn sounds and to travel the world through videos and work in groups.

At community colleges, YouTube is being used in communication courses for public speaking evaluation and feedback. At four-year institutions, instructors are using YouTube to further engage students in a topic that may not be as feasible with a textbook. There are endless avenues in using YouTube as teaching model, so as textbooks become less affordable and less appealing to the next generation of college students, implementing multimedia such as YouTube in the classroom will be the new way of ensuring the academic success of students.

It is equally important for educators who have been in the classroom for years to adopt the technologies. At the rate that technologies are advancing, there is no time for comfort. Instructors need to adopt new technologies and look for ways to be innovative to continue to raise the standards in the classroom.

CHAPTER SUMMARY

- Since YouTube's inception in 2005, it has continued to grow and develop.
- YouTube has become an increasingly vital tool for educators.
- YouTube provides the visual and sound elements that will easily keep the students' attention.
- Four methods are used: flipped instruction, supplemental instruction, self-directed learning, and classroom enhancement.
- At the community college level, YouTube is a reliable source to assist in teaching; however, it comes with some challenges.
- The use of YouTube instruction could help to increase community college enrollment.
- YouTube is used in public speaking courses.
- YouTube can be used effectively in marketing the community college or university.
- At the university level, students like to watch videos which provide an alternative teaching method.
- In some foreign countries, YouTube is used to teach the English language.
- YouTube is evolving as a method to assign oral presentations in class.
- YouTube is being used in online courses.
- YouTube provides access to almost unlimited content.
- Recent figures show that more than half of YouTube views come from handheld devices.
- YouTube videos provide opportunities to expand the understanding of a topic.
- YouTube videos can help instructors provide cultural context to relevant issues in society.
- There are multiple channels dedicated to supporting instructors in art, political science, math, history, and foreign languages.
- As technology advances, so will the expectations of students at colleges and universities.
- It will be important for faculty to learn how to use technology in their courses.
- The YouTube Teacher is a site that shows teachers how to use YouTube in the classroom.
- YouTube videos can work through the flipped classroom approach by allowing learners to digest lecture content at their own pace.

- YouTube allows instructors to fill in gaps with experts that make classroom activities more engaging.
- Instructors must adopt technology in the learning process for the benefit of students.

NOTE

1. Editor's Note: This chapter discusses what has become a 21st-century video library available to anyone. It has a phenomenal variety of topics which can be used in the educational process. Its potential is amazing and will no doubt be used by educators at all educational levels.

REFERENCES

Ace, X. (2016). *The history of YouTube*. Retrieved from https://www.engadget.com.

Alwehaibi, H. (2015). The importance of using YouTube in EFL classrooms on enhancing EFL students' content learning. *Journal of College Teaching and Learning, 12*, 121–126.

Batchelor, D. (2016). *3 reasons to use YouTube in you online class*. Retrieved from https://coursegenius.com/blog/3-reasons-use-youtube-your-online-courses.

Catapano, J. (2018). *Technology in the classroom: Using YouTube*. Retrieved from https://www.teachhub.com/technology-classroom-using-youtube.

Fleck, B., Beckman, K., Sterns, L., & Hussey, D. (2014). YouTube in the classroom: Helpful tips and student perceptions. *Journal of Effective Teaching, 14*, 21–37.

Malouff, J., & Emmenon, A. (2014). Student give psychology away: Oral presentations on YouTube. *Psychology Learning and Teaching, 13*, 38–42. Miami Dade College. 2019. Retrieved from http://www.mdc.edu.

Pedagogical Benefits. 2019. *Institute for teaching and learning innovation*. Retrieved from http://www.uq.edu.au/teach/video-teach-learn/ped-benefits.html.

Staat, D. (2019). *Exponential technologies: Higher education in an era of serial disruptions*. Lanham, MD: Rowman and Littlefield.

YouTube for Educators. 2019. Retrieved from http://www.nea.org/tools/lessons/50803.htm.

Chapter 7

Google Education[1]

Cameron Jackson

Just Google it! Not so long ago, instant access to gigabytes of information via a super computer seemed to be something that would happen sometime in the distant future. Now, average citizens have learned to access information about virtually anything on Google or other search engines via a plethora of smart devices or good old-fashioned personal computers.

The youth of today, Generation Z, were born into a world of Google and the Internet of Things (IoT). This new generation of students is arriving on college and university campuses expecting an engaging learning environment supported by technology. After all, that is how this new generation of students is being taught in the K–12 environment. So, why would it not be the same or better in higher education?

GENERATION Z AND TECHNOLOGY

Michael Dimock, president of the Pew Research Center, wrote that technology in each generation impacts how people communicate and interact (Dimock, 2019). He noted that baby boomers were certainly impacted by the television; Generation X was impacted by computers and video games; and Millennials' communication and interaction was significantly influenced by the advent and expansion of the Internet (Dimock, 2019).

Generation Z was born with television, computers, the Internet; and beginning in 2007, when the first Gen Zers were 10 years old, they had the iPhone. Gen Zer teens all communicated primarily through mobile devices, WiFi, and cellular data. Social media was not a phenomenon Gen Zers had to adapt to as an emerging technology (Dimock, 2019). This was a way of life they were born into and expect. "The implications of growing up in an always on technological environment are only now coming into focus" (Dimock, 2019).

The technology expectations of Gen Zer students are not a passing phenomenon that can be ignored. As of 2018, there were 56.6 million Gen Zers in public school systems and 16.8 million undergraduate Gen Zers in public and private institutions of higher education across the United States (National Center for Education Statistics, 2019). The current and future expectation and demand for technology-supported classrooms will only continue to grow.

GOOGLE FOR EDUCATION

The student-centered, learning-focused, digitally enhanced classroom of the future is already being built today at forward-thinking colleges and universities. The digital classroom of today will continually evolve to keep pace with the emerging technologies of tomorrow. Savvy faculty, staff, and administrators in higher education have already started conversations on campus to better understand how successful colleges and universities must plan and prepare today for the millions of digital natives already funneling onto campus with new expectations for learning from the K–12 pipeline.

Google Education is helping to lead the digital classroom conversation with research, design, rapid prototyping, and collaboration with students and faculty on campuses around the globe. The results of some very exciting case studies and interviews with students, faculty, and industry experts are used throughout this chapter to showcase how a variety of innovative Google tools are being used to enhance teaching and learning. The foundation of Google Education begins in the K–12 environment.

GOOGLE AND K–12 EDUCATION

Enter Google Chromebook. According to Google, the Chromebook is a laptop that uses Google's patented Chrome operating system (OS) and is designed to be used while connected to the Internet using documents and tools in the cloud (Google, 2019). Every Gen Zers is likely to understand what the cloud is, and the first thing to come to mind will likely not be the big fluffy clouds in the sky. The cloud is a network of remote servers hosted on the Internet to store and process digital information, instead of storing and processing data on a personal device.

At the time of this writing, there is a good chance that not all teachers or faculty would immediately think of remotely hosted servers storing and processing data. However, this technology has, in the past ten years, had a significant impact on teaching and learning. It has allowed Google to penetrate the K–12 education environment in an easily deployable and affordable way for school systems.

Charlotte, North Carolina

One of numerous case studies of how Google for Education supported student success in K–12 can be found in Charlotte, North Carolina. The largest single deployment of Google Chromebooks in the world happened at Charlotte-Mecklenburg Schools (CMS). Nearly 150,000 K–12 students in 168 schools took part in this monumental digital learning initiative (Evergreen, 2016). Why? School administrators and teachers at CMS observed what every other school across America experiences—disengaged students.

The answer was to leverage technology in such a way that every student, regardless of socioeconomic status, could access learning resources including computers and educational software in and away from school. Jametta Martin-Tanner, Ridge Road principal, noted that students began to engage in personal responsibility for learning by using the new technology to create weekly learning action plans (as cited in Evergreen, 2016). The results? The CMS four-year cohort graduation rate increased 20% from 2010 to 2016 (Evergreen, 2016).

Union County, North Carolina

Another example of how Google is supporting teaching and learning in K–12 can be found in the Union County Public School (UCPS) system in North Carolina. Casey Rimmer is the director of Innovation and Education Technology for Teaching and Learning in the UCPS system. She and several of her staff were interviewed and provided exciting examples of how they are partnering with Google Education (C. Rimmer, personal communication, April 18, 2019).

This partnership allows UCPS to put digital teaching and learning tools into the classroom as early as the third grade and continue to support the digital learning environment through the remainder of a student's K–12 education journey. The examples discussed later from Casey and her team paint a picture of how a Gen Zers digital native is nurtured and developed in the K–12 system and why there is a student expectation to learn in a digital environment upon arrival at colleges and universities (C. Rimmer, personal communication, April 18, 2019).

UCPS third-grade students are issued Chromebooks loaded with Google G Suite for Education (C. Rimmer, personal communication, April 18, 2019). This tool is supplied to each student for his or her entire K–12 education journey. These tools come to be expected, and eventually demanded as students progress toward high school graduation.

By the sixth grade, students are so familiar with Google's G Suite that they intuitively plan the week, month, and school year using Google Calendar, communicate with other students and teachers using Gmail, and collaborate with other students on assignments using Google Drive, Hangouts, Forms, Sites, Docs, Sheets, and Slides (C. Rimmer, personal communication, April 18, 2019).

Rimmer said teachers have progressively adapted to the new technology-supported teaching and learning environment. Teachers use Google Classroom to organize and post grades and assignments, and to communicate with students. Teachers are encouraged by Rimmer and her staff to use these technologies to facilitate student creativity, collaboration, and teamwork, rather than as a medium of knowledge consumption (C. Rimmer, personal communication, April 18, 2019).

Joey Barker is an instructional coach for UCPS. He explained that the UCPS partnership with Google includes an introduction to technology in a "Walled Garden" or a safe and secure online environment protected through various steps implemented by the Office of Innovation and Education Technology for Teaching and Learning at UCPS. Barker said this digital garden allows young students to safely learn the digital skills that will be used as each student progresses through the school system, and eventually moves into the workforce or higher education where an understanding of how to collaborate and use technology is expected (J. Barker, personal communication, May 30, 2019).

ISTE, North Carolina

Lisa Thompson is on the North Carolina Committee of the International Society for Technology in Education (ISTE). Thompson said introduction of technology at an early age is foundational for teaching young students transferable skills such as collaboration, teamwork, and navigating in a digital learning environment. She said UCPS is introducing technology in the classroom to students early, beginning with iPads in K–2, and issuing all students Chromebooks in grades three through eight (L. Thompson, personal communication, May 30, 2019).

Technological change comes rapidly, and rapid change does not usually come without resistance to adoption and implementation. According to N. Brucia many teachers have welcomed the use of technology in the classroom, but the technology and digital content management has not been easy for all K–12 teachers. Brucia said some teachers are not excited to change the pedagogy he or she has successfully used for decades (N. Brucia, personal communication, May 30, 2019).

Many teachers are excited about the opportunity to engage students in collaborative projects through digital learning tools such as Google Expedition and Google Cardboard. These two examples of Google teaching and learning tools allow students to use virtual reality (VR) headsets to explore hundreds of places on earth to learn about ocean biology, geography, distant cultures, historic events, civil rights, and other lessons (N. Brucia, personal communication, May 30, 2019). However, these amazing learning tools are not meant to replace good teaching (L. Thompson, personal communication, May 30, 2019).

SAMR

A national model has been created to assist teachers with integrating technology into varying spectrums of teaching. The model is called SAMR, which stands for Substitution, Augmentation, Modification, and Redefinition (L. Thompson, personal communication, May 30, 2019). She said the SAMR model helps teachers understand how to incorporate technology such as the Google for Education tools into lessons. "You don't want teachers to use technology to support student consumption of knowledge, the best scenario is for teachers to use technology to help students create something" (L. Thompson, personal communication, May 30, 2019).

NATIONAL RECOGNITION OF THE DIGITAL LEARNER

The two previous K–12 case studies are part of a much larger story of how Google has successfully saturated the K–12 teaching and learning environment with *G Suite* for teachers and students to support classroom management, student collaboration, and creativity. However, Google education tools are not just available to well-funded first world school systems.

Advances in technology and the global proliferation of smart devices put Google tools at the fingertips of everyone with a smartphone. According to the U.S. Department of Education, Office of Education Technology (2019), advances in learning science have resulted in technology enabled learning that allows learners to access digital resources and expertise in his or her own community or around the world (U.S. Department of Education, 2019).

Barriers

Limited resources and geography are less of a barrier today with learner access to high-quality online mentoring and advising programs, digital communication solutions between faculty and students, and more importantly for the topic of this chapter, with mobile data collection tools and online collaboration platforms like Google *G Suite*. For example, schools with connectivity but without advanced science laboratories can engage students in advanced learning opportunities through virtual chemistry, biology, anatomy, and physics labs—offering learning experiences comparable to peer institutions with better resources (U.S. Department of Education, 2019).

Student Interest

Students of all demographics in K–12 and postsecondary institutions have demonstrated an interest in digital learning opportunities and technology-based tools for collaboration, innovation, and individual exploration (Lightle, 2011). The U.S. Department of Education encourages teachers in both K–12 and higher education to use technology to support and enhance learning in formal and informal learning environments (U.S. Department of Education Office of Technology, 2019).

Google for Education enables personalized learning and experiences that are engaging and relevant to groups of students working in collaborative, team-based settings, which is an exemplary model that students will be able to transfer into the workforce upon graduation. Here are a few case studies to help stir the imagination.

CASE STUDIES OF GOOGLE FOR HIGHER EDUCATION

How does Google play a role in supporting teaching, learning, and student engagement in higher education? According to Jamie Casap, Google's Global Education Evangelist (as cited in Kim, 2017) said, "I did not want us to be vendors in the space.... I wanted us to be thought leaders, to have a point of view" (p. 2). Google has an entire team and set of tools to facilitate teaching and learning, collaboration, data recovery, and innovation in the higher education realm. Google for Higher Education team members partner with faculty and students in colleges and universities across the United States. These thought leaders and innovators help faculty create, pilot, and test emerging technologies for the higher education classroom.

Brown University

The first inspiring and creative example of Google for Higher Education comes from an interview with Adam Blumenthal, vice president of Nucco Brain Studio, and Brown University Professor of the Practice for Virtual Reality. Blumenthal has been a producer, designer, and interactive media strategist since 1993. He is part of a VR/augmented reality working group for higher education at Google.

Blumenthal said current students are digital natives that expect to learn by engaging in lessons supported by technology. He believes higher education in general has a problem effectively engaging Gen Zers digital natives in the learning process. His work is about using interactive media to create academically sound and compelling learning experiences that have the look and feel of quality video games. He does not suggest VR or interactive media as the solution, or that it will replace teachers, but he does believe faculty need to supplement textbooks and other older media that students/digital natives struggle with (A. Blumenthal, personal communication, May 28, 2019).

Blumenthal said Google Tilt Brush, Google Daydream, and Google Cardboard are affordable technologies to help faculty use VR to create an interactive higher education classroom in which students are more likely to pay attention, engage in learning, and more easily remember important details about a lesson or topic (A. Blumenthal, personal communication, May 28, 2019). Blumenthal described Google Tilt Brush as a teaching and learning tool that allows students to enter a virtual environment and paint in a 3D space, walking around, painting, or sculpting.

He said Google Cardboard is a cardboard box with two lenses which users hold up to his or her eyes to experience an interactive lesson. The Google Cardboard tool works by inserting a smartphone with a downloaded VR app into a pocket in the front of the device. Google Daydream is also a smartphone supported VR device, but slightly more sophisticated and comfortable than Google Cardboard (A. Blumenthal, personal communication, May 28, 2019).

Blumenthal has used Google Cardboard to create numerous lessons for topics ranging from history to physics. In one instance, he recreated Thomas Edison's lab. He said his students were addressing standards from physics and other courses entering the virtual world. Blumenthal described a virtual environment in which his students could walk around the virtual lab and learn lessons such as how the light bulb was invented (A. Blumenthal, personal communication, May 28, 2019).

Blumenthal's story of how VR can be used in the classroom in an affordable and simple way is only one of several innovative examples of how to use a variety of Google for Higher Education tools. For additional examples of

Professor Blumenthal's use of technology to support teaching and learning, visit https://www.nuccobrain.com/.

Columbia University

Each year Columbia University holds a week-long learnathon and hackathon called DevFest. This event is one of the university's largest tech events, hosting more than 800 undergraduate and graduate students. This tech event includes a week of curriculum content, technical workshops, company sponsors, and lots of prizes (Columbia DevFest, 2018).

Google is one of the company sponsors for this and similar events around the country. Google Cloud Credits can be applied for online and used to support higher education projects at events such as DevFest that are related to student teaching, learning, or research projects that incorporate the Google Cloud application (Google Cloud Credits, 2019).

In this case study, computer science students at Columbia University used Google Cloud Credits at DevFest to develop an app that would allow speech or hearing-impaired people to talk on the phone by converting text-to-speech, and vice versa. The students also used Google Compute Engine's virtual machines. This tool enabled the students to deploy a Flask script that integrated Twilio's voice services with Google's Speech-to-Text and Text-to-Speech APIs to create a relay between voice and text communication (Columbia University Case Study, 2019).

The innovation and creativity of this project demonstrates how resources from Google Cloud Credits, along with a variety of Google tools can be used by university computer science students not only to demonstrate competencies but also to foster an entrepreneurial spirit that supports social sector needs. However, Google for Education is by no means only useful for computer science faculty and students. The next case study from Emory University demonstrates an astounding example of the creative possibilities for Google in higher education.

Emory University

Dr. Shamim Nemati and Dr. Ashish Sharma in the Department of Biomedical Informatics at Emory University's School of Medicine used the Google App Engine to convert a sepsis prediction algorithm into an app that used 30,000 anonymized digital patient health records to analyze 65 variables, such as vital signs, septic patient demographics, and lab results. The artificial intelligence (AI) app created with Google App Engine enabled continuous monitoring of patient data to predict the likelihood of developing sepsis (Emory University Case Study, 2019).

This faculty created app displayed results such as composite sepsis risk scores in a digital dashboard for clinicians to evaluate. It also included an early alert alarm to rapidly notify clinicians of potentially septic patients, potentially saving lives. Faculty designed the app using Google Cloud Platform (GCP) and open-source tools, and now plan to scale the app through GCP and Google Cloud Machine Learning Engine in order to incorporate robust data encryption to patient data and enable expanded use of the app to serve a larger patient population (Emory University Case Study, 2019).

Arizona State University

Students can be very resourceful. Gen Zer students leverage technology as a huge resource on a daily basis. Enter "Team OdySearch" (Alexander Yurowkin, Alexander Shearer, and Sidharth Kulkarni). The three members of Team OdySearch are students from Arizona State University. They were interviewed to learn about how they leveraged Google at a hackathon to provide financial and technological resources for their travel app project called OdySearch.

Team OdySearch was in attendance at a hackathon where representatives from Google Cloud were also in attendance. After a brief explanation of the Team OdySearch project and a short grant application, Google was interested in using the OdySearch app as a use case scenario. Alex, Alex, and Sidharth were given six months to flesh out a prototype (A. Yurowkin, personal communication, June 3, 2019).

The OdySearch is a travel app for students. Yurowkin said his team's app is for college students who have meager budgets but want to travel and see as much as they can. He said "the App works by a student inputting a budget, how much you want to spend, a list of cities to visit, for instance, capitals in Europe, and dates you could potentially travel. The App comes up with potential routes, plane flights, dates, budget, optimizing for price" (A. Yurowkin, personal communication, June 3, 2019).

Team OdySearch said they worked with Google, not with faculty at ASU. However, faculty encouraged the students. The students said companies like Google sponsor hackathons and provide "credits" to use their technology resources to create projects. Team OdySearch said credits with Amazon were used up, so it was incidental that they ended up using Google, who was offering more prizes at the hackathon than any other sponsor. Team OdySearch said the Google product was fairly simple and easy to get and running pretty quickly without issues.

The students said they got lots of internal support from Google engineers (A. Yurowkin, personal communication, June 3, 2019). The students said, "faculty are using outdated methodologies. Most classes forgo innovative tools used in industry. Technology is moving too fast for what academic institutions are doing" (A. Yurowkin, personal communication, June 3, 2019).

Team OdySearch said they give it five years minimum before institutions become serious about high-performance technology-support teaching methods in the classroom. However, they said, "Professors should be current on technologies and try to integrate them into the classroom" (A. Yurowlin, personal communication, June 3, 2019). The next case study is an example of how faculty used Google Education Grants to support engaging classroom projects for students.

City College of New York

Technology changes so rapidly that institutions of higher education often struggle to keep pace with industry. This rapid pace of technological change can create the risk of sending college graduates into the workforce without understanding the latest technology tools and platforms. Faculty at the City College of New York (CCNY) turned to Google to resolve this challenge by applying for a GPC Education Grant to support virtualization and other cloud projects for which learning was not best supported by traditional textbooks and lectures (City College of New York Case Study, 2019).

The GPC Education Grant offered faculty an affordable, practical, and innovative way to give students hands-on experience with industry concepts such as cloud containers and virtual machines, Google App Engine, and Google Compute Engine. Rather than using out-of-date systems purchased by the college, students were able to use up-to-date industry standard systems and platforms through GCP to create innovative and entrepreneurial projects such as machine learning to support optical character recognition of handwriting, or using machine learning to assist physical therapists with helping patients to develop and maintain correct exercise form (City College of New York Case Study, 2019).

The Google for Education team provided these CCNY student project teams with grants of time on GCP to facilitate the development and testing of these class projects. This enabled meaningful and engaging teaching and learning that prepared students for real-world experiences (City College of New York Case Study, 2019). Kudos to the faculty at CCNY for successfully acquiring the resources needed to link theory and practice of application with up-to-date tools used in the workplace.

Georgia State University

Barriers to teaching and learning come in many forms. Access to data during or after a natural disaster is usually not what comes to mind.

However, this is a reality for higher education administrators. Teaching with technology requires reliable and robust resources that can weather the storm. Georgia State's Instructional Innovation and Technology team partnered with GCP to unify data access, security, and storage under the umbrella of Google's remote server infrastructure. This new partnership was tested in September 2017 when Hurricane Irma caused power outages across several Georgia State campuses (Georgia State University Case study, 2019).

According to Kelly Robinson, Director of Enterprise Infrastructure, Instructional Innovation and Technology at Georgia State University, her team was able to quickly bring university systems back online after Hurricane Irma caused prolonged power outages. Robinson said, "While we were able to protect our data before, GCP has made it much easier to perform data recovery after an event like this one" (as cited in Georgia State University Case Study, 2019, p. 1).

Faculty work hard to create meaningful content to engage students. Faculty at many colleges and universities teach some or all courses online for the convenience of students. Using GCP as a disaster recovery tool and backup for faculty lessons and other institutional data can help to limit disruption of teaching and learning. According to Robinson (as cited in Georgia State University Case Study, 2019), GCP was a cost-effective, secure, and convenient option for data recovery and helped move Georgia State closer to a digitally enabled University.

North Carolina State University

Change can be difficult in any organization. Robust technological change is usually very challenging in large organizations. North Carolina State University (NC State) is the largest university in the state with more than 35,000 students and about 8,500 faculty and staff. As one might imagine, collaboration on teaching and learning in an organization of this size can be inefficient and frustrating. The Chief Information Officer (CIO) at NC State thought so too (NC State Case Study, 2019).

The CIO at NC State asked a team to analyze the costs and benefits of several hosted mail, calendar, and collaborations options for students. Testing and student feedback led the university to select Google's *G Suite* as the collaboration tool of choice. This tool was compatible with several of the university's existing software and hardware systems. Many of the students were already using Google tools in K–12. Faculty saw how easily students embraced the transition to Google's *G Suite*. This helped facilitate a smooth cultural shift among both faculty and students toward collaboration within one enterprise solution (NC State Case Study, 2019).

Change management does not always need to be difficult. The fear of technology combined with the fear of change can at times paralyze individuals and institutions. Sometimes the solution is simple. With more Gen Zer students entering the classroom, faculty and administrators may need to turn to tech savvy digital natives (students) to find creative and simple solutions like *G Suite* to move the institution forward.

University of North Carolina at Chapel Hill

The positive impact of scientific research in higher education on society is enormous. However, research can take months and years due to the data-intensive processes. The systems and hardware capable of providing this robust computing power is extensive and expensive. That is why UNC Chapel Hill turned to GCP to accelerate medical research (Chapel Hill Case Study, 2019).

Jeff Roach is the senior scientific research associate for Information Technology Services and Research Computing at UNC at Chapel Hill. Roach worked with Google engineers and Google partner Techila Technologies to improve high-performance computations and data processing for scientific research. Rainer Wehkamp, Techila's CEO, said his company partners with Google because his engineers "believe Google has the most technologically advanced cloud solutions" (as cited in Chapel Hill Case Study, 2019, p. 1).

Roach worked with Wei-Tang Chang, senior research associate of Biomedical Research Imaging at Chapel Hill, to pilot a research project using GPC. The research project used the immense computational power Techila's Computer Engine on GPC to process medical imagery datasets consisting of cortical layers of the brain captured through high-resolution functional magnetic resonance imaging (fMRI). The computational acceleration of Techila and GCP alleviated the wait time of doctors and patients for fMRI image reconstruction (Chapel Hill Case Study, 2019).

According to Roach and Chang, study participants normally go through numerous functional runs, each taking up to 60 minutes, with each image reconstruction taking up to 40 days. This type of research with 20 participants would normally take up to two years. Rather than taking a month to reconstruct, the partnership with Google and Techila enabled UNC Chapel Hill researchers to complete this task in a few hours instead of several weeks, significantly reducing the timeline of the research project (Chapel Hill Case Study, 2019).

Scientific research in higher education is a tremendous benefit to society. Faculty and student researchers can use resources such as the computational acceleration of Techila's Compute Engine on GCP to optimize research and speed up the cycle of moving research and inventions from the laboratory to innovations in the healthcare marketplace. Imagination and creativity seem to be the only limiting factors.

West Point

VR allows users to engage with all the human senses to transform words in a book or faculty lectures into immersive experiences that bring stories alive. This method of learning is memorable and helps participants to pay attention, remember details, and anticipate learning with excitement. This is exactly what Major Antonio "Tony" Salinas did with his cadets at West Point.

Major Salinas is a U.S. Military Academy assistant professor of history who uses his experience in Afghanistan and Iraq to help students understand leadership and teamwork through the lens of historic events. A colleague introduced Salinas to Google Expeditions, which enables faculty to virtually take students anywhere in the world at any time in history (West Point Case Study, 2019). The only limitation is whether or not the program has been written yet.

After prompting from his colleague, Salinas began using Expeditions to teach European History and Western Civilization. He used Google Expeditions to give students a virtually immersive tour of the Gallic War, including Caesar's battles at Alesia, Bibracte, and Gergovia. Salinas said the process of creating lessons in Expedition was pretty easy to learn and did not require the use of expensive equipment. Google Expeditions, a smartphone, and some Google Cardboard (inexpensive Google VR goggles) is all that was needed. Salinas said he plans to create more virtual history lessons for his students using Expedition (West Point Case Study, 2019).

Yale University

This case study demonstrates the broad spectrum of creative teaching and learning possibilities supported by Google for Higher Education. Students at the Yale University School of Arts used Google Tilt Brush to create lifesized VR paintings in 3D spaces. The students were able to reimagine various mediums of art from a completely new 3D perspective (Yale University Case Study, 2019).

Ahanhit Vossoughi is a lecturer and assistant director of Digital Media at the Yale School of Art. In 2017–2018 she introduced VR and Google Tilt Brush to her Visual Thinking and Basic Drawing class. Tilt Brush allowed students to paint in 3D space at room-scale. By doing so, Vossoughi expanded her student's understanding of artistic possibilities. Tilt Brush allows a student to import his or her own original artwork, expand, elaborate, and experiment with the work of art, then export the artwork (Yale University Case Study, 2019).

Once students have learned the basics of introductory drawing, such as line, surface, texture, proportion, perspectives, and other basic drawing concepts, they are then introduced to Tilt Brush and VR. Initial Tilt Brush lessons include an introduction to VR, Tilt Brush controllers, VR headsets, and various brushes, effects, and other art related tools. After this intuitive lesson, students can begin exploring formal artistic elements such as line, shape, color, and texture in a new way (Yale University Case Study, 2019).

The fun really begins for students when they start to understand line and form and to use color theory concepts to modify works. Students can scale up small works into huge pieces in the 3D environment. They can draw on the front or back, turn work around or upside down, export works of art to print, and then in the real world, further expand on the work of art by painting or drawing on what was created in the 3D virtual world (Yale University Case Study, 2019).

The case studies mentioned earlier are only a small sampling of how faculty and students are using Google in creative and innovative ways across a broad spectrum of teaching and learning. The Gen Zers digital native students already come to higher education with an intuitive ability to learn in a technology-supported environment. A starting point for students and faculty who are not sure where to start or where to get resources may be to apply for Google Cloud grants for project-based work.

Interested faculty can just Google examples of research projects that use Google tools to help get the creative juices flowing about how to use technology to engage students in a process that will surely result in positive learning outcomes and improve student success. Learning to teach with technology is the educational barrier that needs to be broken down to advance this engaging form of pedagogy.

TEACHING WITH TECHNOLOGY
IN HIGHER EDUCATION

Dr. Eva Baucom, director of Program Compliance at the nationally renowned School of Pharmacy, at Wingate University in North Carolina, is one of several savvy and forward-thinking higher education experts around the country that understands the need to encourage faculty to creatively use technology such as that offered by Google to support an engaging pedagogy for the higher education classroom of the 21st century. Dr. Baucom asserted that "many faculty in higher education are content experts without formal pedagogical training" (E. Baucom, personal communication, June 3, 2019).

While the desire to teach and impact student success is strong, without training, faculty often revert to the strategy of teaching how they were taught. For many of us, the primary strategy is to lecture with a slide deck. In this model, student "learning" looks quiet: students sit at desks and attempt to write down all of the material they believe will be on an exam, then take an exam. As our learners evolve, higher education must evolve on both the systematic and course levels to meet the needs of our learners. This generation of learners does not know the world without technology, and what do we do in higher education? We take it away, limit their use of it, or use it in non-meaningful ways because it does not fit the model of quiet learning and assessment. Yes, this generation of students has a different skill set than previous generations, but why not build on the strengths that they bring to the table? (E. Baucom, personal communication, June 3, 2019)

Baucom suggested that faculty may recognize the need to evolve, but do not have the training or confidence to change. She said, "if we want our faculty to creatively use technology, we have to provide them with the tools they need to succeed" (E. Baucom, personal communication, June 3, 2019). One of the resources faculty can use as a starting point to better understand how to use tools such as those offered by Google is Bloom's Taxonomy for Digital Teaching.

BLOOM'S TAXONOMY AND DIGITAL TEACHING AND LEARNING IN HIGHER EDUCATION

The advent of digital classrooms and tools such as those offered by Google has led to the creation of a Digital Bloom's Taxonomy (Bloom's Digital Taxonomy, 2019). This new digital taxonomy helps faculty understand how to use digital tools to facilitate learning that results in positive learning outcomes. The purpose of the Digital Bloom's Taxonomy is to demonstrate how to use digital tools "as vehicles for transforming student thinking at different levels" (Bloom's Digital Taxonomy, 2019). The digital taxonomy starts with higher-order thinking skills such as creating, and works downward toward lower order thinking skills, such as remembering (Bloom's Digital Taxonomy, 2019).

According to Bloom's Digital Taxonomy, the most beneficial use of technology in the classroom is as a tool for creation of new or original work (Bloom's Digital Taxonomy, 2019). Digital tools such as Google Cloud, App Engine, Big Query, Firebase, and an extensive list of other powerful Google tools can help students analyze, apply, understand, and remember lessons by engaging in simple or extensive research or other projects with classmates and faculty (Google, 2019). To learn more about Bloom's Digital Taxonomy, check out this link: https://www.commonsense.org/education/videos/blooms-digital-taxonomy

CONCLUSION

The new generation of students dubbed Gen Zers has filled the halls and classrooms on college and university campuses across the globe. These students grew up in a K–12 environment where they were engaged and supported by Google and other technologies. Faculty, staff, and administrators in higher education must continue to engage in conversations to better understand how to plan and implement teaching and learning solutions to engage the millions of digital natives who have new expectations for learning.

Google Education has demonstrated both the willingness and capability to lead the digital classroom conversation. The case studies in this chapter highlight how faculty, students, and administrators can partner with industry experts such as Google to discover what creative and innovative learning can look like on his or her campus. Each case study is as unique as the faculty and students involved.

Using technology to support teaching and learning is not a passing trend. The United States Department of Education encourages teachers in higher education to use technology to support and enhance learning in formal and informal learning environments. Faculty and students who are interested in learning more can discover hundreds of additional case studies online. Bloom's Digital Taxonomy will be helpful too. Just "Google it."

CHAPTER SUMMARY

- Technology in each generation impacts how people communicate and interact.
- The technology expectations of Gen Zer students are not a passing phenomenon that can be ignored.
- The student-centered, learning-focused, and digitally enhanced classroom of the future is already being built today at forward-thinking colleges and universities.
- The foundation of Google Education begins in the K–12 environment.
- Teachers use Google Classroom to organize and post grades and assignments, and to communicate students.
- Technological change comes rapidly, and rapid change does not usually come without resistance to adoption and implementation.

- A national model—SAMR—has been created to assist teachers in integrating technology into varying spectrums of teaching.
- Advances in technology and global proliferation of smart devises puts Google tools at the fingertips of everyone with a cell phone.
- Google for Education enables personalized learning and experiences that are engaging and relevant to groups of students working in collaborative, team-based settings, which is an exemplary model that students will be able to transfer into the workforce upon graduation.
- A number of universities and colleges are working with technology applied to education as revealed in a number of case studies in the chapter.
- A new generation of students dubbed Gen Zers has filled the halls and classrooms on college and university campuses across the globe.

NOTE

1. Editor's Note: This chapter demonstrates the potential of 21st-century technologies when a business, Google, gets involved with learning in a manner compatible with the millennial population who grew up with these technologies. Google is already showing itself to be a leader in what will become another highly successful method of education.

REFERENCES

Bloom's Digital Taxonomy. (2019, June 6). Retrieved from https://www.commonsense.org/education/videos/blooms-digital-taxonomy.

Chapel Hill Case Study. (2019). *At UNC, processing medical images accelerates from one week to three hours*. Retrieved from https://edu.google.com/why-google/case-studies/unc-chapel-hill-gcp/?modal_active=none.

City College of New York Case Study. (2019). Retrieved from https://edu.google.com/why-google/case-studies/ccny-gcp/?modal_active=none.

Columbia DevFest. (2018). Columbia DevFest 2018. Retrieved from https://adicu.com/events/2018S/columbia-devfest-/.

Columbia University Case Study. (2019). *With Google cloud platform, a team of Columbia students help people with disabilities communicate*. Retrieved from https://edu.google.com/why-google/case-studies/columbia-university-nagish/?modal_active=none.

Dimock, M. (January 17, 2019). *Defining generations: Where Millennials end and Generation Z begins*. Fact Tank, News in the Numbers, Pew Research Center. Retrieved from https://www.pewresearch.org/fact-tank/2019/01/17/where-millennials-end-and-generation-z-begins/.

Emory University Case Study. (2019). Retrieved from https://edu.google.com/why-google/case-studies/emory-university-gcp/?modal_active=none.

Evergreen Education Group. (2016). *Impact portraits, success stories with Google for education.* Charlotte-Mecklenburg Schools. Retrieved from https://drive.google.com/file/d/0B__OTXR_u3RbUElRa19QTWZnMlU/view.

Georgia State University Case Study. (2019). Retrieved from https://edu.google.com/why-google/case-studies/georgia-state-university-gcp/?modal_active=none.

Google Cloud Credits. (2019). *Unlock infinite possibilities.* Retrieved from https://edu.google.com/programs/?modal_active=none.

Kim, J. (2017, May 14). *How Google has not taken over the higher Ed classroom: Everywhere, but strangely absent.* Retrieved from https://www.insidehighered.com/blogs/technology-and-learning/how-google-has-not-taken-over-higher-ed-classroom.

Lightle, K. (2011). More than just the technology. *Science Scope, 34*(9), 6–9. Retrieved from https://www.questia.com/library/journal/1G1-270980159/more-than-just-the-technology.

National Center for Education Statistics. (2019). *Fast facts.* Retrieved from https://nces.ed.gov/fastfacts/display.asp?id=372.

North Carolina State University Case Study. (2019). Retrieved from https://edu.google.com/why-google/case-studies/north-carolina-state-university/?modal_active=none.

U.S. Department of Education, Office of Education Technology. (2019). *Engaging and empowering learning through technology.* Retrieved from https://tech.ed.gov/netp/learning/.

West Point Case Study. (2019). *West point professor leads cadets onto Caesar's ancient battlefields with Google expeditions.* Retrieved from https://edu.google.com/why-google/case-studies/west-point/?modal_active=none.

Yale University Case Study. (2019). *Yale University art students explore painting in 3D with VR and Tilt Brush.* Retrieved from http://services.google.com/fh/files/misc/yale_case_study.pdf.

Chapter 8

MOOC Education[1]
Angela Davis

Online education has become one of the most common modes of learning for students. With roots in business and industry, massive open online courses (MOOCs) have expanded their reach into all levels of the education system. This chapter will define MOOCs, explore its strengths and weaknesses, and outline how MOOCs should be implemented in higher education. The chapter will conclude with exploring why students are attracted to this teaching method and why MOOCs would work successfully in higher education in the 21st century.

MOOCS DEFINED

Introduced after the Open Education Movement, MOOCs began in 2008 when a group of 25 Siemens employees enrolled in a fee-based course. The course was eventually made available to other registered learners resulting in over 2,300 people participating in a course without paying registration fees (Yuan & Powell, 2013). The phenomenon grew as other institutions of higher education became interested in the idea. In 2011 scholars at Stanford granted admittance to an online course that sparked the interest of over 160,000 learners globally.

During the past decade, MOOCs have become an Internet sensation where learners from all backgrounds can access education for free. MOOCS are usually comprised of video lectures, online discussion boards, and slideshows (Hoy & Brigham, 2014). Registration is easy and courses begin as soon as the student has enrolled. While the student is taking the course, online quizzes test the knowledge of the learner. As unemployed and underemployed workers seek industry credentials for better paying careers, online learning has become an affordable and accessible way to achieve this goal.

MOOCS ONLINE

The online experience for student learners participating in a MOOC method of learning is different from other online course environments. MOOCs require that students are actively engaged by creating and sharing with an online learning group (Hollands & Tirthali, 2014). Although it appears that colleges and universities are seeing an increase in MOOC registration, there is little research to support high completion rates. Institutions of higher learning must weigh the costs of offering MOOCs versus the traditional seated or hybrid teaching methods (Hollands & Tirthali, 2014).

While some scholars believe that MOOCs will revolutionize the way formal education is delivered, others view this dramatic method of learning as a step backward. Critics believe that the delivery of methods of videos and online tests do not allow the student to retain the information learned from the course (Ostashewski & Reid, 2012). Research also shows that there are two types of MOOCs: the AI-Stanford MOOC and the Connectivist or c-MOOC (Ostashewski & Reid, 2012).

The MOOC and c-MOOC methods are both free to learners, have expert practitioner instruction, and run over a sequence of weeks (Ostashewski & Reid, 2012). Differences lie in the role of the instructor. The AI-Stanford MOOC assumes a conventional lecture style of spreading knowledge to the student. The c-MOOC assumes a personalized learning approach that embraces opposing and creative thinking, allowing learners to collaborate, connect, and share (Ostashewski & Reid, 2012).

UNIQUE FEATURES OF MOOCS

According to Ostashewski and Reid (2012), George Siemens, one of the creators of the c-MOOCs, developed eight features that make the c-MOOC unique:

1. Connectivist in nature where knowledge is distributed and that learning is the process of navigating, growing and pruning connections;
2. Knowledge is generative as opposed to replicative as in the AI-MOOC model which results in learners creating and sharing digital artifacts;
3. Coherence (of the topic being studied) is learner formed as a result of the learner exploring the topic and related domains of knowledge—as

opposed to an instructor controlling what materials will be explored in the study of the topic;
4. Interactions are distributed across the networks and tools employed;
5. Synchronization of learners and their knowledge is facilitated by all those participating;
6. Resonance or "idea collision as innovation" with other learners occurs;
7. Innovation & impact focused; and
8. Fostering self-regulated learners (Ostashewski & Reid 2012, p. 2).

The c-MOOC model provides support for student learning using social media and technology. Unfortunately, many institutions find it hard to assess student outcomes from MOOCs.

Universities and colleges are not the only educational institutions interested in MOOCs. According to Chlonda Claude, consultant for exceptional children for schools in North Carolina and Virginia, teachers and students in elementary, middle, and high schools across the country are also intrigued by the learning method. In the K–12 system, MOOCs are moving traditional classrooms to a flipped learning model where students have the flexibility to access resources at home before coming to class (C. Claude, personal communication, June 11, 2019).

Having access to large amounts of online educational resources is beneficial to all teaching methods. Many teachers in K–12 see the benefits of MOOCs and describe them as the future of education. In contrast, recent surveys also show that many teachers believe that MOOCs devalue the educational system and view them as a downfall (Brahimi & Sarirete, 2015).

FOUNTAIN FORT CARSON HIGH SCHOOL

Harry Knight, the STEM Coordinator for Fountain Fort Carson High School located in Fountain Colorado believes that MOOC models only work for students capable of handling the rigor and self-discipline of the online learning environment. Some young scholars struggle with the online model and need instructors to hold their hand step-by-step. While other students prove to be successful using this learning model because of their already existing study habits (H. Knight, personal communication, July 16, 2019).

According to Harry Knight, the Fountain Fort Carson School District #8 was the first high school district in Colorado to pilot this model of learning. The school district worked with a team of teachers, parents, and students to pilot MOOCs. Fountain Fort Carson High School has been using this model for 10 years (H. Knight, personal communication, July 16, 2019).

MOOC FLEXIBILITY

Many students prefer MOOCs because of the flexibility and the opportunity to get ahead by working at their own pace. In order to fully execute this type of learning model and integrate it into an established culture of learning, instructors must be engaged. Some instructors give limited online feedback, while others take the time to fully participate with the student in this community of practice (H. Knight, personal communication, July 16, 2019).

To assist students without WiFi, the high school has invested in a five-mile WiFi antenna to provide WiFi access to all students in the district. The school district has also partnered with the local library to remove barriers to technology access. The local library has extended their hours of operation so that the computer lab is available for students who do not have laptops or Internet access (H. Knight, personal communication, July 16, 2019).

The school district has also received grants to provide laptops to students and their parents. The grants also fund training for parents on how to use computer technology and support their student learner (H. Knight, personal communication, July 16, 2019). Currently, every student in Fountain Fort Carson School District #8 has access to laptops.

MOOCS STRENGTHS

Scholars support the benefits of MOOCs in higher education. According to Yuan and Powell (2019), MOOCs help to guarantee access to education but must include future changes to see the following positive outcomes:

1. Globalization and the increased momentum for internationalization in higher education;
2. Worldwide growth and increasing demand for access to higher education, with the projection that there will be 120 million students worldwide by 2020;
3. Changing learner demographics, experience and demands of the dramatically increasing numbers of lifelong adult learners;
4. Highly increased access to personal technology and social media; and
5. The need for changes in cost, affordability and economic models for higher education. (Yuan & Powell, 2019, p. 15)

Students from all backgrounds can participate in MOOC programs, allowing participants to join an open and evolving learning model.

This emerging trend requires the need for instructors to participate in professional development to learn more about this learning model (Viswanathan,

2014). Instructors are also encouraged to use this model in order to become well-connected 21st-century educators and better equip students for the career of their choice.

Students with Disabilities

While there is limited instructor interaction, some students with disabilities may benefit from MOOCs. The ability to complete the course at a student's own pace can support the accommodation of extended time in traditional classroom settings. A student with this type of accommodation benefits by reducing the anxiety associated with having to complete assignments or tests in a short period of time. This flexibility may enhance the learning for some students with disabilities (C. Claude, personal communication, June 11, 2019).

Learning is stimulated when students share their opinions with everyone, while engaging with others during MOOC sessions. MOOCs provide a space for students to learn the importance of accountability and taking responsibility for their overall learning experience (Viswanathan, 2014). MOOCs provide a platform that reaches students across the globe.

MOOCS WEAKNESSES

MOOCs can oftentimes present some challenges. During a recent study to evaluate the effectiveness of MOOCs, Viswanathan (2014) outlines the following challenges:

1. Limitations in sharing information with insufficient comprehension,
2. Low Internet connectivity and inability to participate in webinars at times, and
3. Limitations in the applications of learning inputs in all types of teaching and learning environments. (p. 37)

To eliminate barriers, providing laptops or computer access may not be enough. Tackling the barrier of low Internet connectivity may require local government and industry collaboration. Varying budgets and community college demographics can limit applications of learning as some colleges may not have the funding to purchase programs used in some MOOCs (Viswanathan, 2014).

Access Issues

World access to the Internet remains a problem. It is estimated that only one-third of the world's population has access to the Internet. This is quite different for some European countries, the United States, and Canada where Internet usage surpasses 80% (Sanchez-Gordan & Lujan-Mora, 2019). Although the Internet usage in the United States is higher, rural communities still have Internet access issues which create barriers to education.

According to Ostashewski and Reid (2012), there are risks associated with MOOCs. These include the following:

1. Risks around "open" resources,
2. Return on development costs,
3. Controls of learner engagement, assessment and tracking of learners, and
4. Scalability of interactions. (Ostashewski & Reid, 2012, p. 4)

Some of these risks could be lessened using organizational, operational management, and learning analytics tools for the delivery of MOOCs (Ostashewski & Reid, 2012).

The National Center for Education Statistics found that over 200,000 students entering college in the fall of 2017 had some type of learning disability. Many believe that MOOCs cannot stand alone for special education students. Special education students are best served when there is a combination of flip model and traditional teaching (C. Claude, personal communication, June 11, 2019).

For exceptional children (EC) students, MOOCs give the student more autonomy by allowing them to work at their own pace and access instruction when they are not in school. The student is able to go back and review content when the teacher is not around. This also allows parents to assist their student more readily because they can see the instruction for themselves (C. Claude, personal communication, June 11, 2019).

However, EC students still require adult interaction so that there is someone to see how they are perceiving instruction and how they are using resources. There has to be direct instruction on using MOOC systems so that EC students understand how to capitalize on those resources (C. Claude, personal communication, June 11, 2019).

DROPOUT RATES

Dropout rates are high for students who enroll in MOOCs. The researchers also noted that the past actions of students will predict their future outcomes. There is value in predicting the persistence rates and drop rates of students. One benefit is that instructors can identify the barriers and activity patterns these students may face and develop strategies for student retention (Halawa, Greene, & Mitchell, 2014).

The flow of influence design can provide understanding about the academic patterns of students.

Halawa et al. (2014) believe that in order for an intervention model to be effective and action based, an instructor must be able to know the following:

1. Who is at risk of dropout and who is not: If the model cannot accurately identify high-risk students, then instructors obviously run the risk of sending interventions to the wrong students; and
2. When the student activity starts exhibiting patterns predictive of dropout: The sooner we can detect dropout risk, the sooner we can intervene. If an intervention is sent too late, it may be less effective. (Halawa et al., 2014, p. 5)

While having the information may prove valuable, there is still little data to support its benefit.

COMMUNITY COLLEGES

Dr. Susan Paris, chief academic officer at Durham Technical Community College, says MOOCs may not be the best idea for community colleges. When MOOCs were first rolled out at Durham Tech in 2011, the vision was to bring free education to the underserved, community colleges' largest student population. Enrolling students in massive MOOCs at no cost, for the purpose of obtaining credentials and/or degrees is a heavy sell. She does not believe MOOCs have come through on their promises (S. Paris, personal communication, July 18, 2019).

Sanchez-Gordan and Lujan-Mora (2019) stated that the Obama Administration viewed MOOCs as the answer to the world's knowledge divide, yet MOOCs have not yet delivered on that promise. All education, in every form, should be encouraged; unfortunately, MOOCs have not met the goals they were designed to meet (S. Paris, personal communication, July 18, 2019). Most students need the guidance of an instructor and the support of classmates to bring their best thinking to their studies. Self-paced learning requires incredible discipline, which MOOCs cannot provide (S. Paris, personal communication, July 18, 2019).

Best Served Students

MOOCs still exist of course, but are no longer as massive. They can provide an alternative for a particular type of student—one who is incredibly self-motivated, is not looking for a traditional degree, and does not want to pay even a small fee for their education. MOOCs fail to educate a community of diverse people, which remains the mission of community colleges (S. Paris, personal communication, July 18, 2019). MOOCs can also be viewed as a threat to brick-and-mortar colleges and universities (Yuan & Powell, 2014). The future of MOOCs could support the online university and college movement, whereby posing a threat to the traditional education model.

FEARS ABOUT MOOCS

The central and fundamental services of education are shifting and colleges are having challenges with the shift to MOOCs. Colleges and universities are fearful that MOOCs will threaten the financial stability and sustainability of the traditional campus educational model (Mazoue, 2019). The following new and innovative trends pose a challenge to brick-and-mortar institutions:

1. The emergence of the learning sciences and their application to educational practice;
2. The movement toward competency-based education; and
3. New business models that effectively combine instructional quality, lower cost, and increased access through unlimited scalability. (Mazoue, 2019, p. 2)

When MOOC programs become credit-based and result in an accredited degree from colleges and universities, this will shift the mindset regarding the acceptance of the teaching model (Mazoue, 2019).

IMPLEMENTING MOOCS IN HIGHER EDUCATION

According to Viswanathan (2014), MOOCs could be offered self-sufficiently at the university or college level to enhance students' academic performance. Viswanathan (2014) suggests the following:

1. The online courses could be offered to a set of students who require individual attention;
2. Instructors can promote the use of digital literacy among students by encouraging them to actively participate in online discussions during classes and interact with their peers through social networking sites like Twitter or Facebook; and
3. Instructors can work on their professional development by updating their knowledge of specific subjects and offer MOOCs frequently relating to those subjects of specialization. (p. 4)

It is further noted that supplementing classroom instruction with MOOC sessions urge students to actively take part in learning and collaborating with others (Viswanathan, 2014).

University of Colorado

MOOCs have been offered in the University of Colorado educational system since 2013. These courses are offered through Coursera and are at zero cost to participants (H. Knight, personal communication, July 16, 2019). MOOCs teach students how to become lifelong learners, while helping instructors improve their professional skills (Viswanathan, 2014).

Durham Technical Community College

According to Timiya McCormick, online education specialist at Durham Technical Community College, the college has been offering online courses since the mid-2000s. The vendors that support the college's online programs are Education to Go, LERN-UGotClass, and the American Management Association. None of these courses are free and fees can range from $70 to $5,000 depending on the course and the credential the student is trying to obtain (T. McCormick, personal communication, July 18, 2019).

The college averages close to 700 registrants for online courses through third-party vendors annually. Currently, the college is seeing a 90% completion rate for these types of classes. Students enrolled in these courses come from all backgrounds and demographics. The ages range from 16 to 70 and students have all levels of educational backgrounds, including doctoral degrees (T. McCormick, personal communication, July 18, 2019). Pursell, Zhang, Jablokow, Choi, and Velegol (2016) found MOOC students were over 30 years of age, with a postsecondary degree.

Hollands and Tirthali (2014) state that institutions of higher learning have different opinions on integrating MOOCs into their systems. Some colleges are creating MOOC courses that are tailored to fit the needs of their student population. Some colleges are also using MOOCs developed by other colleges and universities. Most college and universities are waiting to see outcomes from other institutions before they consider the MOOC model (Hollands & Tirthali, 2014).

Colleges and universities also find it difficult to engage faculty in the MOOC discussion. Community colleges are becoming engaged and have developed MOOCs that meet the needs of their diverse population of students. Hollands and Tirthali (2014) also noted that many colleges and universities are integrated MOOCs into their flipped classroom models or as additional resources for their students.

Hollands and Tirthali (2014) conducted a study to gain information about MOOCs by interviewing various individuals in public and private, two-year institutions, four-year institutions, researchers, online learning platform providers, for-profit education companies, and various stakeholders in the online learning community. Over 62 institutions were interviewed for the study and nearly half of the participants were already offering MOOCs. The results outlined the following institutional goals:

1. Extending the reach of the institution and access to education;
2. Building and maintaining the brand;
3. Improving economics by lowering costs or increasing revenues;
4. Improving educational outcomes for MOOC participants and on-campus students;
5. Innovation in teaching and learning; and
6. Research on teaching and learning. (Hollands & Tirthali, 2014, p. 6)

The research also showed potential savings related to development and delivery of MOOCs. In the past MOOCs strained institutions financially, but participants in the study offered possible solutions for cost saving measures: reusing MOOC materials multiple times; sharing MOOC materials across instructors and campuses; developing common courses to offer across institutions; replacing on-campus courses with MOOCs; saving faculty time; reducing the need for facilities; creating recruitment efficiencies; and developing less costly student support services provided by non-faculty members (Hollands & Tirthali, 2014).

MOOC Instructors

Hollands and Tirthali (2014) found that most participants believed that in order for MOOCs to be successful, instructors must reframe how they instruct. The participants in the qualitative study offered suggestions on how to improve the educational outcomes of students:

1. Provide instant feedback to course participants;
2. Gamification and badging to increase motivation;
3. Outreach to MOOC participants to encourage persistence; (Add "Provide") Adaptive learning, personalization, or mastery-based learning;
4. Flipping the classroom using MOOCs to provide the online content;
5. Motivating instructors to rethink pedagogy;
6. Redesigning regular courses to incorporate MOOC strategies, such as "chunking" lectures and interspersing questions, and increasing opportunities for peer-to-peer learning;

7. Using MOOCs in K–12 to prepare students for college; and
8. Fine-tuning instructional materials. (Hollands & Tirthali, 2014, pp. 10–11)

MOOCs could theoretically decrease the costs of higher education if they are used to remove the duplication of comparable courses across campuses. (Hollands & Tirthali, 2014)

MOOCs and Student Engagement

MOOCs would be very beneficial for the community college to offer to students (T. McCormick, personal communication, July 18, 2019). Most of the students currently enrolled in our third-party online courses are able to afford the fees associated with the course. Unfortunately, the majority of the students the college serves are unable to pay for an education because they are either unemployed or underemployed (T. McCormick, personal communication, July 18, 2019).

The majority of our scholarship programs do not assist students in paying for MOOC courses. Some of our community partners offer scholarships for unemployed or underemployed citizens. MOOCs would be an economical choice for individuals who cannot afford go to school (T. McCormick, personal communication, July 18, 2019).

Wang and Baker (2015) conducted a study to evaluate the motivations of learners when taking a MOOC course. Reviewing a course offered through Coursera, one of the main MOOC platform vendors, the researchers studied if the motivations of students were related to completion (Wang & Baker, 2015).

Students with learning goals have more motivation to succeed. Learning goals assist students with increasing competence and overall performance (Wang & Baker, 2015). Access to a brick-and-mortar institution also encourages students to utilize the MOOC model. Students who are not geographically located near a traditional college or university often seek online platforms to access high education.

MOOC Completion Status

The MOOC status of completion may differ from the traditional student success in a traditional seated course (Pursell et al., 2016). Traditional success is defined by a grade that indicates a student has successfully passed the class (Pursell et al., 2016). For student who takes MOOCs, success may be defined as the following:

1. The ability to interact with peers interested in the same content; or
2. Learning a single concept (out of several) covered in a MOOC. (Pursell et al., 2016, p. 214)

According to Pursell et al. (2016), the MOOC model is well-liked by non-native English speakers even though the MOOC was developed in English. Scholars also identified that it was more probable that non-native English speakers complete the MOOC course over native English speakers (Pursell et al., 2016). Researchers also concluded that non-native English speakers may prove to be more probable to complete MOOC courses because the achievement holds more significance globally, where the opportunity to secondary education is problematic. Using MOOCs is a way to 'sample' American academic institutions (Pursell et al., 2016).

MOOCS, HIGHER EDUCATION, AND 21ST-CENTURY TECHNOLOGIES

In the book *Exponential Technologies: Higher Education in an Era of Serial Disruptions*, Darrel Staat (2018) states that the most students are familiar with the college courses related to 20th-century technologies. However, with the development of new technologies, community college leaders must become more concerned about the effect they will have on higher education. Unfortunately, educational systems are proving an inability to keep up with the exponential technological growth (Staat, 2019).

The changes in the fourth industrial revolution will require businesses to participate in ongoing training in order to stay relevant (Staat, 2019). Although many community colleges are embracing a meta-major pathway model, continuing education can prove to be an asset in this new way of thinking to enhance student performance. MOOCs can help bridge this gap.

College leaders must develop a growth mindset in order to adequately and rapidly prepare for the growth of new technologies. It will be essential for college leaders to inform all stakeholders in order to successfully deal with the rapid change (Staat, 2019). Traditional strategies will prove to be stagnant as technology grows exponentially.

With the development of new technologies, community college leaders must become more concerned about the effect they will have on education (Staat, 2019). Bold moves and creativity will be necessary and in collaborating with new industry partners to stay on target with the exponential growth. Community college systems will need to evaluate state budgets in order to assist with developing new training. The flexibility and accessibility of MOOCs can complement the creativity needed to develop courses for jobs of the future.

CONCLUSION

The Internet has always provided a global gateway to education, thereby creating an autonomous process of making the knowledge of mankind available to all people (Hoy & Brigham, 2014). Since 2008, institutions of higher learning have started offering courses online in a range of formats (Hoy & Brigham, 2014). MOOCs are online classes that use the worldwide web to offer education to everyone everywhere. In the world of MOOCs there are no more boundaries.

MOOC student learners can receive a certification of accomplishment once the course is successfully completed (Fifilia & Pardamean, 2016). MOOCs test the knowledge of students using tutorials, tests, quizzes, online community engagement exercises, and final examinations (Fifilia & Pardamean, 2016). According to researchers, there many advantages and disadvantages to the MOOC model. MOOCs provide flexibility and convenience and student learners can complete the courses at their own pace (C. Claude, personal communication, June 11, 2019). However, the model calls for students to be disciplined and self-motivated to complete the course.

The growth of MOOCs and online learning is happening at a fast pace. The technologies of the 21st century are growing exponentially (Staat, 2019). MOOCs and online learning can impact that technological development and innovation in education by providing accessible courses to prepare the global workforce for the jobs of the future.

CHAPTER SUMMARY

- With roots in business and industry, MOOCs have expanded their reach into all levels of education.
- MOOCs are usually comprised of video lectures, online discussion boards, and slide shows.
- Although it appears that colleges and universities are seeing an increase in MOOC registration, there is little research to support high completion rates.
- In addition to higher education, MOOCs are used in the K–12 system allowing students to have access to resources before coming to class.
- Some young scholars struggle with the online model and need instructors to hold their hand step-by-step.
- On the other hand, many students prefer MOOCs because of the flexibility and the opportunity to get ahead by working at their own pace.
- Students from all backgrounds can participate in MOOC programs, allowing participants to join an open and evolving learning model.

- World access to the Internet remains a problem.
- Dropout rates are high for students who enroll in MOOCs.
- MOOCs can provide an alternative for a particular type of student—one who is incredibly self-motivated, is not looking for a traditional degree, and does not want to pay even a small fee for their education.
- College and universities are fearful that MOOCs will threaten the financial stability and sustainability of the traditional campus educational model.
- Colleges and universities also find it difficult to engage faculty in the MOOC discussion.
- MOOCs would be very beneficial for the community college to offer students.
- Students with learning goals have more motivation to succeed.
- The changes in the fourth industrial revolution will require businesses to participate in ongoing training in order to stay relevant.
- The flexibility and accessibility of MOOCs can complement the creativity needed to develop courses for jobs of the future.

NOTE

1. Editor's Note: MOOCs are another pathway to learning at the higher education level. This method began in 2008 with a great deal of fanfare. Over the years it has become less successful than it was originally thought to be; however, it is far from being defunct. MOOCs will most likely evolve into a highly accepted method of teaching and learning.

REFERENCES

Brahimi, T., & Sarirete, A. (2015). Learning outside the classroom through MOOCs. *Computers in Human Behavior, 51*(B), 604–609. doi: 10.1016/j.chb.2015.03.013.

Fifilia, X., & Pardamean, B. (2016). MOOC model: Dimensions and model design to develop learning. *The New Educational Review, 43*(1), 28–40. doi: 10.15804/tner.2016.43.1.02.

Halawa, S., Greene, D., & Mitchell, J. (2014, March). *Dropout prediction in MOOCs using learner activity features*. Retrieved from https://oerknowledgecloud.org/sites/oerknowledgecloud.org/files/In_depth_37_1%20(1).pdf.

Hollands, F., & Tirthali, D. (2014). Why institutions offer MOOCs? *Journal of Asynchronous Learning Networks, 18*(3). doi: 10.24059/olj.v18i3.464.

Hoy, M., & Brigham, T. (2014). MOOCs 101: An introduction to massive open online course. *Medical Reference Services Quarterly, 33*(1), 85–91. doi: 10.1080/02763869.2014.866490.

Mazoue, J. (2019, July 15). *The MOOC model: Challenging traditional education.* Retrieved from https://www.edcause.edu/ero/article/mooc-model-challenging-traditional-education.

Ostashewski, N., & Reid, D. (2012). *Delivering a MOOC using a social networking site: The SMOOC design model.* Retrieved from https://espace.curtin.edu.au/bitstream/handle/20.500.11937/28872/189357_72449_71610_Pub_Ver.pdf?sequence=2&isAllowed=y.

Pursell, B. K., Zhang, L., Jablokow, K. W., Choi, G. W., & Velegol, D. (2016). Understanding MOOC student: Motivations and behaviors indicative of MOOC completion. *Journal of Computer Assisted Learning, 32*, 202–217. doi: 10.1111/jcal.12131.

Sanchez-Gordan, S., & Lujan-Mora, S. (2019, June 30). *MOOCs gone wild.* Retrieved from https://desarrolloweb.dlsi.ua.es/moocs/moocs-gone-wild.

Staat, D. (2019). *Exponential technologies: Higher education in an era of serial disruptions.* Lanham, MD: Rowman and Littlefield.

Viswanathan, R. (2012). Teaching and learning through MOOC. *Frontiers of Language and Teaching, 3*, 32–40.

Wang, Y., & Baker, R. (2015). Content or platform: Why do students complete MOOCs? *MERLOT Journal of Online Learning and Teaching, 11*(1), 1–18.

Yuan, L., & Powell, S. (2019, June 30). *MOOCs and open education: Implications for higher education.* Retrieved from https://publications.cetis.org.uk/wp-content/uploads/2013/03/MOOCs-and-Open-Education.pdf.

Chapter 9

Virtual Reality Education[1]
Darrel W. Staat

In 1957 a transistor was placed on a chip the size of a thumbnail. It took little more than a decade for one transistor on a chip to morph into over 2,000 transistors on a chip in the early 1970s. Vacuum tubes had seen their day. During the 1960s, Moore's Law stated that the number of transistors on a chip was doubling every two years. By 2019, Intel had placed 100 billion transistors on a thumbnail size chip. Over the years, that exponential growth rate resulted in the development of transistor radios, personal computers, smartphones, Facebook, Twitter, Uber, Airbnb, and a host of other digital developments, including virtual reality (VR).

> Anyone who hasn't paid attention to Mark Zuckerberg spending billions to acquire Oculus Rift or Apple's many purchases of augmented reality-focused companies is doing themselves a disservice. If you're in a position to get your hands on a VR headset, then you should, if only to get a taste for its current applications and its future implications. (Scoble & Israel, 2017, p. xvi)

VIRTUAL REALITY

VR has been around in various forms since the 1980s with games played with a head mounted display (HMD) that put one into a reality that was virtual in nature. The headset shut out the real world for the time it was worn, and a virtual world came into view. To begin with it was simple, but it existed. As Moore's Law accurately predicted the increase of transistors per chip, the HMDs improved with clarity and realism; so much so that by 2019 the world of VR is all around, above and below the person with the headset. No matter the direction turned horizontally or vertically, the virtual world is accurately there.

"Virtual reality has one goal: to convince you that you are somewhere else" (Parisi, 2016, p. 2). When a person places the headset properly on the head, the eyes see a three dimensional world that is so accurate, that the individual feels the environment. It is as if the person is actually there. "When this is done right, our brain becomes confused enough to treat these signals as reality" (Bailenson, 2018, p. 51). It is vastly different from watching a movie on a flat screen when the real world is still all around and the difference is easy to comprehend. Wearing a headset that blocks out the real world and allows the wearer only to see the virtual world is totally different.

Virtual comprehended as real is phenomenal. Here is "an artificial environment that is experienced through sensory stimuli (such as sights and sounds) provided by a computer and in which one's actions partially determine what happens in the environment" (Merriam-Webster.com, n.d. as cited in in Donnally, 2018, p. 7). What the individual sees and hears virtually actually appears real. That has tremendous potential for learning. It allows the student to be transported to almost anywhere to see and hear exactly what could be seen and heard as if the student were actually there.

Quarterback Training

The use of VR is limited only by the imagination. Already many companies have developed programs that can be used for educational purposes. A fascinating example was training for a professional football quarterback who learned to react much faster to game possibilities after watching and listening to virtual games that had been videoed (Bailenson, 2018). Without the interference of the real world, the quarterback could concentrate on the game to learn what he could do in future situations to become more successful. He could watch the game virtually over and over, which provided his mind with increased reflex possibilities that he could and did use in real football games (Bailenson, 2018).

Welding Training

Another example was in use at the Southeastern Institute of Manufacturing and Technology (SiMT) located on the campus of Florence Darlington Technical College in Florence, South Carolina. Welding training for potential employees at a local business was provided at SiMT. The company had found that real training in a welding lab resulted in taking a great deal of time, a loss of material, and significant costs for instruction. SiMT provided virtual training in a lab using HMD and physical wand. The students donned HMDs and found themselves in what looked like a real welding facility (M. Roth, personal communication, October 5, 2019).

There were what appeared to be pieces of steel that needed to be welded together. The students took the wand in hand and held it next to the two pieces of metal to be welded. When they pressed a button on the wand, it appeared that the welding began. The students moved the wand down the space between the two pieces of virtual metal and by doing so learned the proper hand movements to make to weld the pieces together. When they finished, the computer revealed how accurately they had completed the weld. If the weld were not done properly, the student could try repeatedly until the weld was completed correctly.

When the student met the course objectives and went to work at the business, it was found that the virtual training they had received worked very well in the real welding world. The business was happy with the results, and the students were employed, meeting the goals of both the company and the students. Virtual learning is a real possibility, which undoubtedly will become a boon to business and industry in a variety of occupations. The potential for the future of education is tremendous.

Public School Education

VR is being used in public schools in Fitchburg Massachusetts (Thompson, 2018). The school system has integrated VR in eight different schools ranging from elementary to high school. The teachers use virtual field trips to bring the students to far off places that they would be unable to access such as a desert, rainforest, tundra, or the Northern Lights. In some cases teachers created their own field trips by recording such things as the monarch butterfly migration. They got an Iditarod dog sled racer to film the experience, which the teachers converted into VR for the student's use (Thompson, 2019).

Nursing Training

The University of Michigan's graduate nursing program found VR as an excellent training program for its students. "You can't be around a bleeding-out patient until a patient is actually bleeding out, so a virtual experience where you could see what's going on could be amazing" (University of Michigan: Virtual Reality, 2019). Since those in the nursing profession must learn how to deal with patients who may possibly die without help, learning how to deal with them in a virtual manner allows the students to learn and practice the skills needed before dealing with an actual patient. The potential for learning using VR is tremendous.

DEVELOPMENT FOR EDUCATION AND TRAINING

VR brings a method that can be developed by teachers and used by their students. No doubt, students will soon be developing VR presentations themselves, since most of them already have smartphones with video capabilities. In ten years, this method of instruction could exponentially grow and become integrated into education at all levels from elementary school to graduate education. It will place student learning at the center of education. Faculty will become learning managers, guides, and problem solvers. Students will learn by doing. The potential is there and is developing in a linear manner at present; however, an exponential explosion is just around the corner.

To take this a step further, there are predictions that in a very few years, the headset will shift from bulky headsets to eyeglasses which will look like normal eyeglasses but with have the full ability of today's PC or cell phone. Instead of carrying the computer in one's pocket or purse, the computer power will be integrated into eyeglasses (Scoble & Israel, 2017). Individuals will use their eyes to control the computer which will be used similarly to the way the PC or cell phone is used now for everything for games, shopping, researching, learning, and the like.

ISSUES WITH VR

Although VR has phenomenal potential for education, there is evidence already that there could be problems as well as types of unanticipated side effects. Jeremy Bailenson (2018) points out that using VR can cause tiredness and pain. His research has found that people do best if they use an HMD for a limited amount of time of about 20 minutes. Because VR creates an alternative world that the individual is involved in and one which the person actually feels emotionally, it makes sense to use the technology carefully and for short periods of time. The brain could be affected to the point where the VR world almost becomes the real world and that possibility could cause real problems for the user.

In addition, there is the problem of eye fatigue, which could create issues in seeing when the user removes the HMD. "Young children are, for instance, notoriously susceptible to acquiring false memories when exposed to everything from verbal narratives to mental images to altered photographs" (Bailenson, 2018, p. 72). As VR becomes more popular and used in a wider variety of settings, more of its adverse effects may become evident and will have to be dealt with.

A barrier for using VR in education at the moment is the extreme cost in purchasing the equipment. The highest quality HMDs cost in the range of $300–$1,000 dollars and, in addition, most need a high-powered computer in addition to operate them. Some use wires from the computer to the headset, which creates mobility issues for the user. Others are wireless, which is the format that future developments will undoubtedly use.

HMD DEVELOPERS

As of this writing the frontrunners in the HMD world are Oculus Rift, HoloLens, and HTE Vive. All are a long way down the road to developing high-quality headsets and each of them are continuing to develop their particular products to the maximum. Others in the field are moving forward significantly, and more companies will join the fray in the future. Investors are already placing billions of dollars in the development of VR technology.

The costs will decrease in the near future due to demand and the ever-increasing computer power as a result of Moore's Law. The day of a classroom filled with high-quality HMDs are a few years off, but getting to understand the possibilities of VR makes it worthwhile for secondary schools, community college, and universities to make a purchase of a few HMDs to begin to learn how the technology could best be used for instructional purposes.

For educators interested in the potential of VR in the classroom and lab, there are a number of organizations that are already developing possibilities for the technology including foundry 10.org, subvrsive.com, mutualmobile.com, merge.com, frulix.com, and more on the Internet. The number of companies will increase significantly over the next decade as this technology takes on a life of its own in education, business, and entertainment.

CONCLUSION

It must be remembered that this technology, still in its infancy, will have to be watched and studied continuously to determine its possible deleterious effects as well as its potential positive impacts. At the moment, the positive seems to far outweigh the negative. Compare it to the Internet, which brought an amazing number of positive effects, while at times, has shown some negative impacts as well.

CHAPTER SUMMARY

- In 1957 one transistor was placed on a chip the size of a fingernail; in 2019, Intel placed 100 billion transistors on a chip.
- VR improved tremendously from the 1980s to 2019 with clarity and realism.
- Wearing a VR headset blocks out the real world and replaces it with a virtual world that is totally different.
- VR has tremendous potential for learning.
- The uses of VR are limited only by the imagination.
- VR has been used to improve a football quarterback's skill level, teach students how to weld, bring virtual field trips to K–12 schools, and improve nursing education.
- Within the next ten years VR will grow exponentially and become integrated into education from elementary school to the doctoral level.
- During the next decade it is possible that the large headsets now being used with VR will become something that looks like a normal set of eyeglasses.
- There are potential problems and unanticipated side effects connected to VR.
- As of this writing the frontrunners in the HMD world are Oculus Rift, HoloLens, and TE HTE Vive.
- As HMDs become more cost effective, a classroom filled with high-quality HMDs are just a few years off.
- A number of companies are already developing possibilities for VR use in education.
- VR Education is in its infancy at the moment, but is potential is amazing.

NOTE

1. Editor's Note: Although virtual reality (VR) has been around for decades in the game world, recent increases in computer power have brought this format to the attention of those in education from kindergarten to the doctoral level. Currently, the development for VR use in education is just getting off the ground. Future potential for the process is unbounded.

REFERENCES

Bailenson, J. (2018). *Experience on demand: What virtual reality is, how it works, and what it can do.* New York, NY: W.W. Norton & Company, Inc.

Donnally, J. (2018). *Learning transported: Augmented, virtual and mixed reality for all classrooms.* Portland, OR: International Society for Technology in Education.

Parisi, T. (2016). *Learning virtual reality: Developing immersive experiences and applications for desktop, web, and mobile.* Sebastopol, CA: O'Reilly Media, Inc.

Scobel, R. & Israel, S. (2017). *The fourth transformation: How augmented reality and artificial intelligence change everything.* Pembroke Pines, FL: Patrick Brewster Press/Novel Rank.

Thompson, M. (2018). Making virtual reality a reality in today's classrooms. Retrieved from https://thejournal.com/articles/2018/01/11/Making-Virtual-Reality-a-Reality-in-Today's.

Virtual reality: From Everest to the OR. (2019). Retrieved from https://michigantoday.umich.edu/2019/09/26/virtual-reality.

Epilogue

Teaching in the 21st century will undergo significant and, in some cases, exponential changes over what has been successful pedagogy in the previous century. What worked well in the classroom and lab from kindergarten to doctoral studies will soon go by the board as the use of technologies become widely used. The movement from a teacher-led focus to a student-learning focus will demand different ways of developing education.

Technology will be used to assist and support the faculty and at the same time provide students with a wide variety of pathways to learning. Faculty will need to learn the new possibilities for the student-focused learning. Some in the teaching ranks will find the new methods easy to learn; others may find it very difficult. The goal of this book is to bring to the foreground ways that can be used to facilitate the change in how education will develop in this century.

The possibilities discussed in this book are only the beginning; obviously as time moves on more concepts will be created and implemented, some with success, others left by the wayside. Rapidly changing technologies will push change in the educational realm far beyond anything seen in the 20th century in order to meet the demands of business and life in general in the 21st century.

About the Editor

Dr. Darrel Staat began his career in education in 1964 as a teacher in a Junior High School. When those students graduated from high school, they invited him back as their graduation speaker even though, after obtaining his master's degree, he had left the school and gone on to teach in a community college. After completing his doctorate, he shifted to community college administration gradually moving up in duties, responsibilities, and accomplishments.

In 1991 he assumed his first presidency of three community colleges, one of which he was founding president. After 19 years in the position of college president, he assumed the position of president of the South Carolina Technical College System. Following his retirement, he returned to teaching as assistant professor and coordinator of the Higher Education Executive Leadership Program at Wingate University, where he is in his sixth year as of the publication of this book.

Dr. Staat is concerned about the future of higher education as it collides head-on with the developments of technologies during the 21st century. His research on the future of higher education led to the publication of four books, including this one, all of which have to do with different aspects of the impact of 21st-century technologies on higher education.

About the Contributors

Angela Davis holds a master's degree in business administration and an EdS in higher education administration. She is currently the special assistant for equity and inclusion at Durham Technical Community College in Durham, North Carolina.

Cameron Jackson holds a master's degree in public administration, a master's degree in international affairs, and an EdS in higher education administration. He is currently the assistant vice president for auxiliary services at Wingate University in Wingate, North Carolina.

Antonio Jefferson holds a master's degree in science in higher education administration and an EdS in higher education administration. He is currently a director of Lyceum and multicultural programming at Wingate University in Wingate, North Carolina.

Melisa Johnson holds a master's degree in educational accommodation and an EdS in higher education administration. She is currently the dean of arts and sciences at Northeastern Technical College in Cheraw, South Carolina.

Linda Latham holds a master's degree in adult education, a master's in nursing education, and an EdS in higher education administration. She is currently a dean of health technologies at Forsyth Technical Community College in Winston-Salem, North Carolina.

Don Miller holds a master's degree in fine arts, a master's degree in English, and an EdS in higher education administration. He is currently the dean of the Learning Commons at Piedmont Community College in Roxboro, North Carolina.

Maria Williams holds a master's degree in public administration, a master's degree in postsecondary education, and an EdS in higher education administration. She is currently the employment assistant coordinator for Career Services at Greenville Technical College in Greenville, South Carolina.

www.ingramcontent.com/pod-product-compliance
Lightning Source LLC
Chambersburg PA
CBHW030141240426
43672CB00005B/212